Get Ahead in Chinese

中学阶梯汉语
A Chinese Course for GCSE

第一册 主编 宣力
Lik Suen

Vol.1

CYPRESS BOOKS

CYPRESS BOOK CO. UK LTD.

Get Ahead in Chinese Vol. 1
By Lik Suen

Editor: Jing Ru
Cover Design: Wenqing Zhang

First published in Great Britain in 2008 by Cypress Book Co. UK Ltd.
13 Park Royal Metro Centre
Britannia Way
London NW10 7PA

Tel: 02084530687
Fax: 02084530709
Email: info@cypressbooks.com

Find us at www.cypressbooks.com

Text copyright©2008 by Lik Suen

The moral rights of the author have been asserted.

All rights reserved. No part of this publication may be reproduced or transmitted by any means, electronic, mechanical, photocopying or otherwise, without the prior permission of the publisher

ISBN 978-1-84570-005-8

Printed in China

About the Author

Lik Suen is Senior Lector in Chinese in the Chinese Department, School of Oriental and African Studies, University of London.

She is a graduate of Beijing Language and Culture University (BLCU) and has an MA in Chinese Linguistics from Hong Kong.

She has 15 years experience of teaching Chinese as a foreign language at schools and universities in China's mainland and Hong Kong, USA and UK. She also taught methodology, pedagogy and linguistics on the teaching training programme at the Chinese University of Hong Kong.

She is a national examiner for the Mandarin Proficiency Test (PSC) of the People's Republic of China and held an equivalent examiner position in China's Hong Kong. She is also Chief Examiner in Chinese for a major examining group in UK.

Preface

Get Ahead in Chinese is designed to help students achieve their potential as language learners, enabling them to overcome the inherent complexity of Chinese and reach GCSE and equivalent proficiency through a new approach to learning.

The distinctive features of this series of textbooks are:

The students are active participants in the language learning process, playing the main role in exploring, discovering and practising the language. The teacher's role is to support students by providing examples of correct pronunciation, vocabulary and grammar, while assessing their progress.

The students learn to use Chinese characters from the very first lesson; pinyin supports this process, but is rapidly phased out. Vocabulary and grammar are built up systematically throughout the book. Character practice and a high frequency of repetition ensure students to better recognize and memorize Chinese characters. Students who follow this approach tend to move ahead of those who stick with pinyin during the second year of study.

Get Ahead in Chinese systematically covers grammar and vocabulary and aims to enable the student's to communicate with Chinese about the things they find mutually interesting, to travel in China as a tourist and to provide a basis for future study and employment.

From the first unit the learners develop all four language skills, listening, speaking, reading and writing. Each unit contains three activities which reinforce learning points through realistic tasks, topics and settings.

How to use this book:

Each task starts with listening. After listening to the recording of the text, the teacher should allow students enough time to figure out the meaning of new vocabulary by themselves. Solutions to the vocabulary exercise in the textbook are provided in the following recording.

Oral practice is important. Students should be encouraged to speak as much as they can.

The new characters in each character practice section are allowed to be photocopied and used as flashcards.

The Compiler
March 2008

前 言

　　《中学阶梯汉语》是一套从零起点开始的初级中学汉语教材，适合海外及国际学校的非母语学习者使用。全套书共分四册，前三册为主体教材，第四册为复习册。在校学习者可望在二至三年修毕全套教材。本教材具有以下主要特点：

- 在功能上采用了欧洲框架，涵盖了初级到中级的相关语用要求。
- 在话题选择方面，既包括海外中学生的日常活动，又紧贴中国现实，多元化地介绍中国的文化与生活。
- 在语言技能的培养方面，听说读写四项技能平衡发展，力求学生做到四能：能听，能说，能读和能写，以达到交际及应试的要求。
- 在编写理念方面，鼓励学生成为主动学习者，去发现和使用中文，因此在课文和练习编写时，遵循少讲多练的原则，安排符合中学年龄段学习心理的语言练习。
- 教材以汉字教学为核心，考虑到中学教学时数的限制，教材严格控制每课的新字量，通过增加汉字的复现率以及各种类型的书写练习，帮助学生克服汉字记忆难的问题。
- 全套教材教授约八百个汉字，其中第一册的汉字量为一百八十一个，第二册为二百二十二个，第三册为二百八十五个。第四册为综合复习册，除整合前三册的语法词汇外，还补充了相当数量的基础汉字和词汇。

　　希望这套教材达到和满足您的学习要求。我们热切盼望您的反馈意见与批评指正。

编者
二零零八年于伦敦

Contents

UNIT	TOPIC	TASK		PAGE
Unit 1 第一单元	Welcome 欢迎	• Task 1 • Task 2 • Task 3 • Task 4	China Chinese language and cities Chinese characters Pinyin	1 3 5 11
Unit 2 第二单元	Introduce Myself 我是……	• Task 1 • Task 2 • Task 3	你好 我姓王 我的电话是……	20 23 27
Unit 3 第三单元	My Family 我的家人	• Task 1 • Task 2 • Task 3	他们是我的家人 她不是我妹妹 我家有两只狗	33 36 40
Unit 4 第四单元	The Family 家人	• Task 1 • Task 2 • Task 3	你叫什么？ 我妈妈是老师 男老师很爱喝英国茶	47 52 55
Unit 5 第五单元	My Birthday 我的生日	• Task 1 • Task 2 • Task 3	八月七号是我的生日 今天是星期天 我问你	60 64 68
Revision Unit 1				74
Progress Test 1 (Unit1T1-Unit4T1)				77
Progress Test 2 (Unit1T1-Unit5T3)				80
Unit 6 第六单元	Directions and Time 方向和时间	• Task 1 • Task 2 • Task 3	他们是中国人吗？ 现在几点？ 英国现在是晚上九点半	83 87 91
Unit 7 第七单元	School（Ⅰ） 学校（一）	• Task 1 • Task 2 • Task 3	我们都喜欢吃中国饭 我的中学 这是我的时间表	96 101 105

UNIT	TOPIC	TASK		PAGE
Unit 8 第八单元	School（Ⅱ） 学校（二）	● Task 1 ● Task 2 ● Task 3	校长会说中国话 教数学的是高老师 学校有一个新图书馆	111 115 119
Unit 9 第九单元	Hobbies 爱好	● Task 1 ● Task 2 ● Task 3	我最喜欢的运动是打球 学生没有时间看电视 最好吃的中国饭	123 127 132
Unit 10 第十单元	Daily Routine 日常生活	● Task 1 ● Task 2 ● Task 3	很忙的中学生 告诉爸爸妈妈学校的事情 你应该学一点儿中文	137 141 145
Revision Unit 2				150
Progress Test 3 (Unit1T1-Unit6T3)				154
Progress Test 4 (Unit1T1-Unit8T3)				159
End of Book I Test (Unit 1-Unit 10)				164
Exercise Answers				169
Appendix I Vocabulary				182
Appendix II Extra Vocabulary				193
Appendix III Fixed Expressions				194
Appendix IV List of Chinese Characters				196

Unit 1

Welcome 欢迎

In this unit you will learn:

- information about China, Chinese language, Chinese characters, and Chinese pronunciation
- numbers 0 to 10
- how to write Chinese characters

Task 1   China

Location and national flag

 China is located in East Asia, with Russia and Mongolia to the north, Pakistan and India to the west, Thailand and Vietnam to the south, with Korea and Japan to the east. The national flag has five stars on a red background.

The highest mountain in the world

Mount Everest, with a height of 8,844 metres (29,017 ft) is situated at the edge of the Tibetan Plateau (Qing-Zang Gaoyuan), on the border between Nepal and China.

China descends in elevation step by step from the west to the east. Mountains and hills make up 69.4% of the total area, including 6 other mountain peaks reaching higher than 8,000 metres.

Size of China

The total area of China is 9,596,960 sq km.
- Similar in size to the United States;
- About 40 times the size of the United Kingdom;
- Sichuan, one province in central China which is famous for its spicy cuisine, is as big as France with a population of more than 100 million.

Economic growth

The annual economic growth rate has stood at more than 7% since 1995.

Currency

The Chinese currency is called Renminbi (RMB), meaning "people's currency". Units of RMB are popularly referred to as *yuan*. One *pound* is equal to about 14 *yuan* (2008).

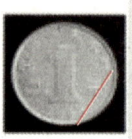

Ex. 1.1   Answer the following questions about China.

1. Name 4 neighbouring countries of China:
   _____, _____, _____ and _____.

2. The colour of the national flag is _____. There are _____ stars on it.

3. The highest mountain, Mount Everest, is _____ metres tall, i.e. _____ feet.

4. What is the total area of China in sq km ?

5. What is the name of the Chinese currency? £100 can buy how many *yuan* at present?

Task 2   Chinese language and cities

Chinese language

Chinese is one of the 5 working languages of the United Nations.

The national language is Putonghua (普通话, common speech) or Mandarin. This is also called Guoyu (国语) in the Taiwan area and Huayu (华语) in Singapore and Malaysia. As a written language, Chinese has been in use for over 4,000 years.

Putonghua is used as a spoken language in more and more areas in China. Most people who live in areas where different dialects are spoken can also understand Putonghua.

Southern Chinese have a long tradition of working overseas and Chinese immigrants have built up Chinatowns around the world, such as those in London, Manchester, Los Angeles, New York and Vancouver.

Cantonese is one of the local dialects of southern China and is widely used in overseas Chinese communities. "Dim sum" is a typical Cantonese food.

As a working language in the United Nations, Chinese has the most users in the world. About 1.5 billion people in the world speak Chinese.

Population and cities

China has about 22% of the total population of the world. Its population reached 1.3 billion in 2006. Eleven cities have a population of over 2 million, including Beijing, Shanghai and Hong Kong.

The following map shows some cities in China.

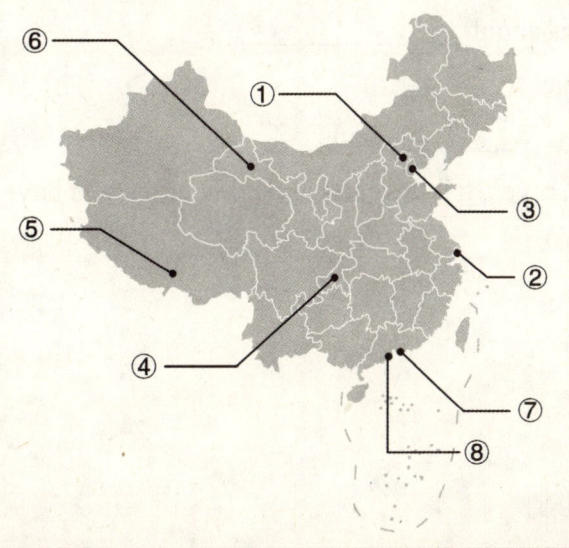

- ① **Beijing** (北京) is the capital of China and has many historic and scenic sites attracting many visitors.
- ② **Shanghai** (上海) is a major port and the biggest commercial city in China.
- ③ **Tianjin** (天津) and ④ **Chongqing** (重庆) are two cities that are also municipalities directly under the central government.
- ⑤ **Lasa** (拉萨), known as **Lhasa**, is the provincial capital of the Tibet Autonomous Region at an altitude of 3,650 metres.
- ⑥ **Dunhuang** (敦煌) was an important junction on the ancient Silk Road. This ancient route from China to the Mediterranean has served as a highway for merchandise as well as for religious and cultural ideas since the 5th century AD.
- ⑦ **Xianggang** (香港), known as **Hong Kong**, was governed by the United Kingdom for about 100 years before it was handed back to China in 1997.
- ⑧ **Aomen** (澳门), known as **Macao**, was governed by Portugal, and was given back to China in 1999.

Ex. 1.2   Questions about Chinese language and cities.

1. The national language of China is _____.
2. What is the most commonly used Chinese dialect in overseas Chinese towns? _____.
3. The population of China is about _____.
4. Name 4 big cities in China:
   _____, _____, _____ and _____.
5. Have you been to China? If yes, tell the class about the cities you have visited.

Task 3   Chinese characters

Knowledge about Chinese characters

Chinese characters are used for written Chinese and have influenced the Japanese and Korean scripts.

You can read a newspaper if you know 3,000 characters.

The sound of a Chinese character can vary in different dialects, but in each dialect it usually has the same meaning.

Some characters are pictograms, but in modern Chinese more than 80% of characters are composed of one phonetic component and one meaning component.

In China's mainland, simplified Chinese characters were introduced in 1956 to help reduce mass illiteracy. They are widely used in China's mainland, Singapore and overseas Chinese communities.

Traditional characters are still used in Hong Kong and Taiwan.

The following are some of the ancient types of Chinese characters.
(a) Oracle Bone Script (1600 BC – 1046 BC)
(b) Bronze Script (1122 BC – 256 BC)
(c) Seal Script in the Qin Dynasty (221 BC – 206 BC)

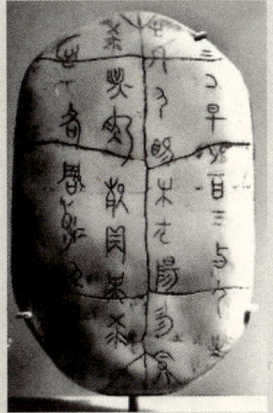 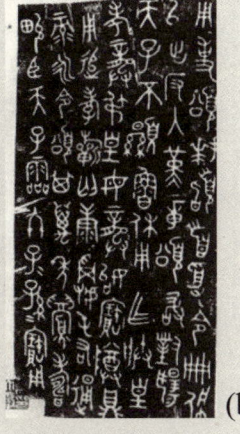 

(a)   (b)   (c)

Look at the table on page 6. You can see how the character "dragon" has gradually evolved over 4,000 years from Oracle Script, to Bronze, to Bamboo, to Seal, to Clerk, to Traditional, and to Simplified version.

甲骨文　　金文　　楚简文字　　小篆　　隶书　　楷书　　简体楷书

Ex. 1.3　Now, can you guess the meaning of the following characters?

	Oracle	Today's character	Meaning		Oracle	Today's character	Meaning
1.		日		2.		月	
3.		山		4.		水	
5.		火		6.		马	
7.		羊		8.		牛	
9.		家		10.		龟	

Chinese characters and their strokes

All Chinese characters are built up from basic strokes.

The simplest have only one stroke while the more complex characters can have more than 20 strokes.

The following table in Ex. 1.4 will show you how to write the strokes and how they are put together to make different characters.

Unit 1
Welcome 欢迎

Ex. 1.4   Stroke practice. Fill in the strokes in the boxes. Pay attention to the direction.

Stroke	Direction	Name	As in						
、	○	Dot	火 羊	○	○	○	○	○	○
一	→	Horizontal	羊	—	—	—	—	—	—
丨	↓	Vertical	羊 山	丨	丨	丨	丨	丨	丨
丿	丿	Curve left	月 家 牛	丿	丿	丿	丿	丿	丿
、	、	Curve right	火 水	、	、	、	、	、	、
乛	乛	Horizontal plus vertical	日 月	乛	乛	乛	乛	乛	乛
亅	亅	Vertical plus tick	小 水	亅	亅	亅	亅	亅	亅

Ex. 1.5   Character practice. Copy the following characters 4 times each on a piece of paper. Make sure you are following the stroke orders the directions showing.

Meaning	Today's character		Oracle Script
▶ Left vertical stroke before top horizontal stroke			
mouth	口 (with stroke order 1, 2, 3)	丨 冂 口 丨 冂 口	⊔

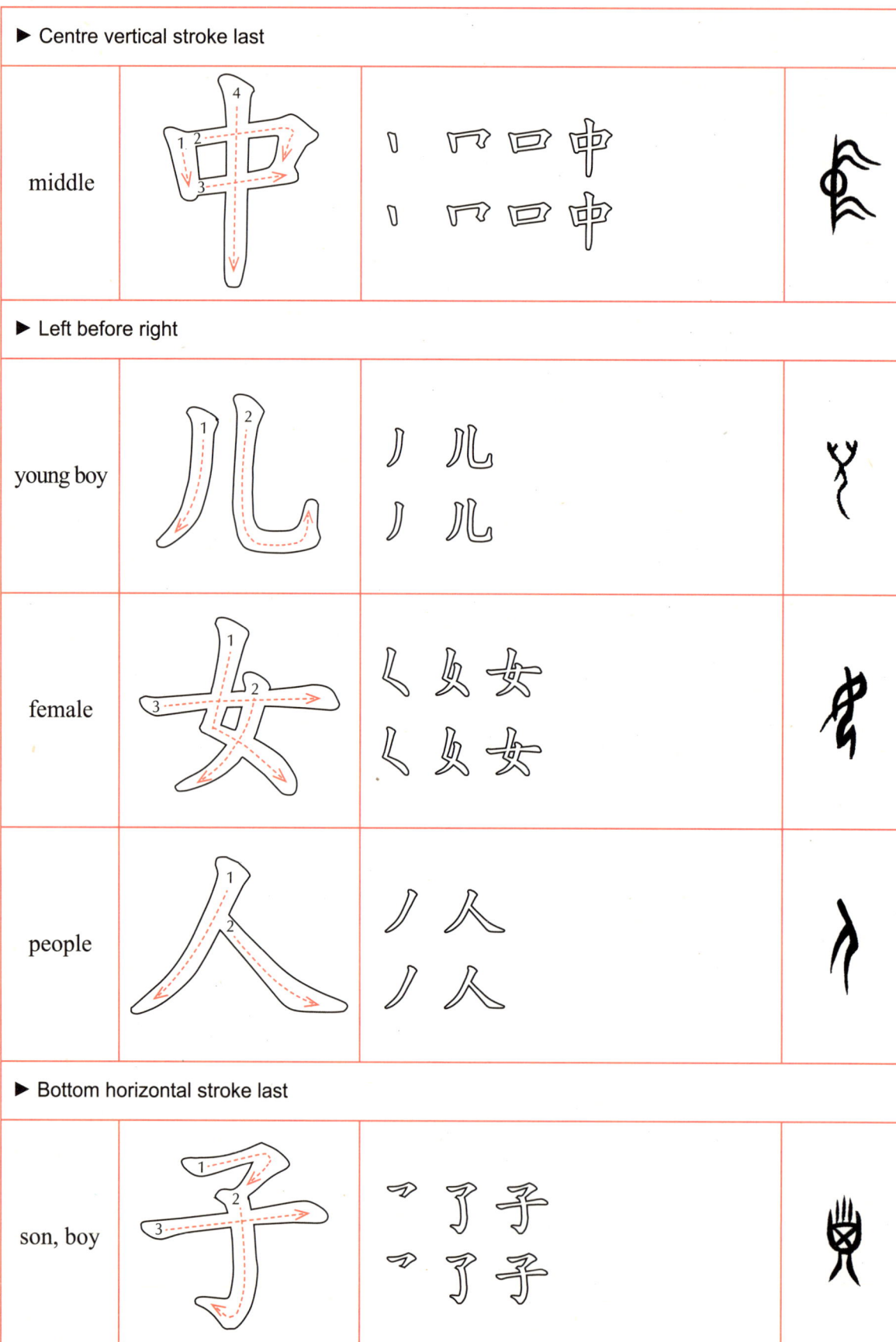

Unit 1
Welcome 欢迎

▶ Horizontal strokes before interesting vertical strokes

big	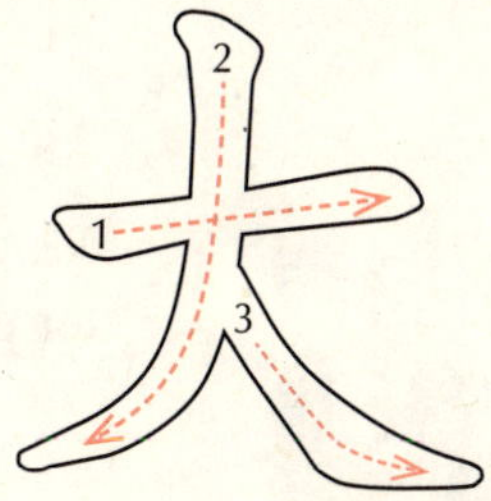 大	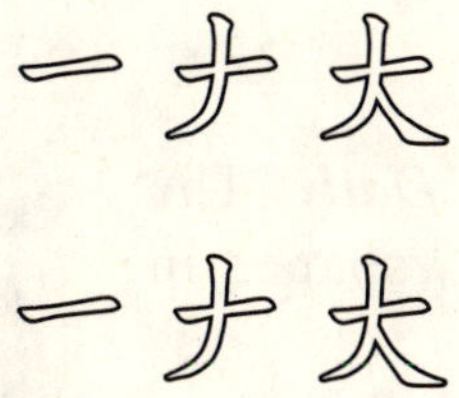 一 ナ 大 一 ナ 大	
heaven, sky, day	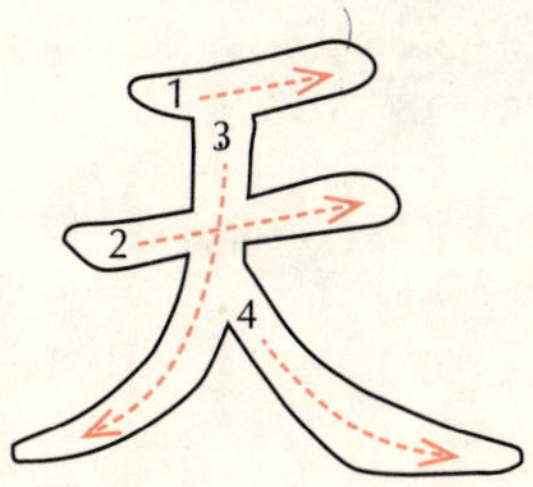 天	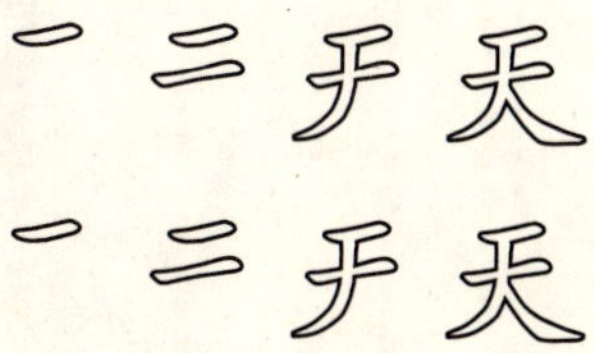 一 二 于 天 一 二 于 天	

▶ Centre stroke before wings

little, small	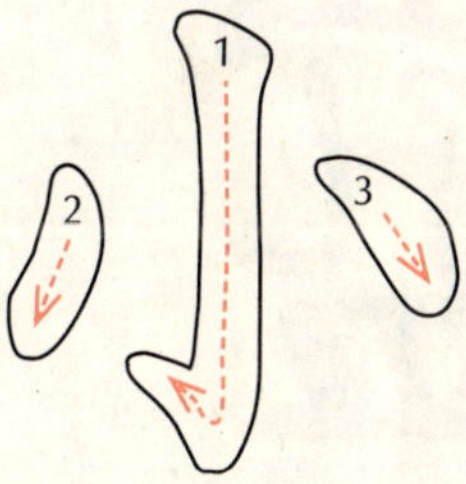 小	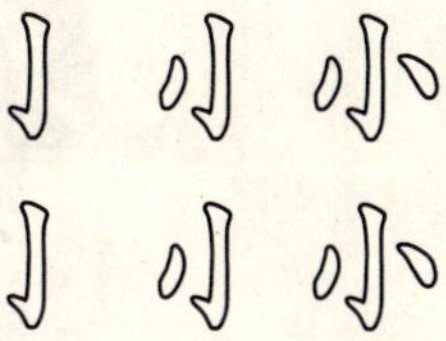 亅 小 小 亅 小 小	

▶ Top before bottom

home, family	 家	 丶 丶 宀 宀 宀 宀 宀 宀 家 家	

Chinese characters and Chinese people's daily life

Chinese characters are used in Chinese people's daily life. The following examples are a newspaper, a Chinese painting and an example of calligraphy.

People's Daily: The main newspaper in China
《人民日报》

Mountain and water painting

山水画

Chinese calligraphy
中国书法

Ex. 1.6 These are the characters you've already been introduced to in this task. Can you guess their meanings?

1. 日　　2. 月　　3. 马　　4. 儿　　5. 家

6. 龟　　7. 火龙　8. 女人　9. 儿子　10. 女儿

11. 子女　12. 家人　13. 小牛　14. 小羊　15. 山火

16. 火山　17. 大人　18. 水牛　19. 山羊　20. 人口

Unit 1
Welcome 欢迎

Task 4   Pinyin

Pinyin

Pinyin is a system of writing Chinese in the Roman script that we use for English and other European languages.

It was created and introduced in 1958 as a method of Chinese phonetic instruction. Today, it has been accepted as the preferred transcription system for Mandarin.

However, Chinese people use characters rather than Pinyin in their daily life. Pinyin is treated as a useful tool in helping students to learn the sounds of Chinese characters.

There are 23 beginning sounds called initials, 37 ending sounds called finals and 4 tones in the Pinyin system. Initials and finals combine with tones to create the meaning and sound of a Chinese syllable. Most sounds of Pinyin are very similar to English. Only a few sounds require special attention.

Quick guide to Chinese initials

b as p in sPy	c as ts in leT'S
p as p in Pet	s as s in Silk
m as m in My	j as j in Jeep
f as f in Fun	q harder than ch in CHeap
d as t in sTy	x sounds between See and She
t as t in Turn	zh as g in George
n as n in New	ch as ch in CHat
l as l in Light	sh as sh in SHoe
g as g in Girl	r as r in Read
k as k in King	w as w in Work
h as h in Hot	y as y in You
z as ds in kiDS	

Quick guide to Chinese finals

a as in bAR	er as in bIRd
ai as in pIE	i as in sEA
an as in bAN	ia as in YAH
ang as in hUNG	ian as YEN
ao as in mOUth	iang as YOUNG
e as in thE	iao as in mIAOW
ei as in sAY	ie as in YEllow
en as in tEN	in as in YO
eng as in ERNG	ing as in sING

iong as in YOONG
iu as in hUgh
o as in sAW
ou as shOW
u as in gOOd
ua as in noW ARm
uai as in WHY
uan as in ONE

uang as in WANder
ui as in WAY
un as in WON
uo as in WAR
ü as in French tU
üan as in YOU ANger
üe as in YOU Egg
ün as in UNited

Ex. 1.7   Now, read out the following syllables.

1. ben   dou   peng   ming   nin   wang   pao   pan
2. hei   gen   ying   pu   nan   wan   gou   rang
3. can   zen   shang   san   zai   chang   ren   tou
4. she   tiao   qin   can   cai   xu   qiang   shi
5. zi   jiu   zhi   si   xie   qiao   ci   chi

Ex. 1.8   Listen carefully and choose the right Pinyin spelling for the eight Chinese cities.

1. 北京 A. Baijin   B. Peking   C. Beijing
2. 上海 A. Shanhai   B. Shanghai   C. Sanhai
3. 天津 A. Tanjin   B. Tianjing   C. Tianjin
4. 重庆 A. Chongqing   B. Chongking   C. Chongqin
5. 拉萨 A. Lasa   B. Lasha   C. Lesa
6. 敦煌 A. Duanhuang   B. Dunhuang   C. Danhang
7. 香港 A. Xianggang   B. Hong Kong   C. Xianggan
8. 澳门 A. Aomun   B. Aomen   C. Oumen

12

Unit 1
Welcome 欢迎

Chinese Tones

Chinese is a tonal language, and there are four tones used in Putonghua (Mandarin). The patterns of the four tones are shown with their pitches below.

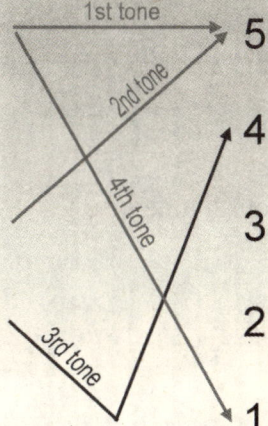

- 1st tone "ˉ": A high and flat tone.

- 2nd tone "ˊ": A rising tone. Compare with surprising "How?" in English.

- 3rd tone "ˇ": A combination of a low falling and then rising tone. Compare with a questioning "Well?" in English.

- 4th tone "ˋ": a high falling tone. Compare with "Done!" in English.

Tone marks are added to the main vowels in Pinyin. For example:
ā ǒ é ī ù ǔ

Ex. 1.9 Let's learn the pronunciation of the characters that have already been introduced. They are grouped by tones.

1st: 天 tiān 家 jiā 中 zhōng 山 shān 龟 guī

2nd: 牛 niú 羊 yáng 儿 ér 人 rén 龙 lóng

3rd: 口 kǒu 水 shuǐ 火 huǒ 子 zǐ 女 nǔ
     小 xiǎo 马 mǎ

4th: 日 rì 月 yuè 大 dà

Ex. 1.10 Now, let's learn the numbers in Chinese. Listen to the recording carefully and repeat.

0	1	2	3	4	5	6	7	8	9	10
líng	yī	èr	sān	sì	wǔ	liù	qī	bā	jiǔ	shí
〇	一	二	三	四	五	六	七	八	九	十

Ex. 1.11 Written exercise. Now listen to the recording again, can you add the correct tone marks above the vowels of each Pinyin?

First tone: (—)   yi (1)   san (3)   qi (7)   ba (8)

Second tone: (´)   ling (0)   shi (10)

Third tone: (ˇ)   wu (5)   jiu (9)

Fourth tone: (`)   er (2)   si (4)   liu (6)

Ex. 1.12 Challenge question.

1. In the UK, which numbers are unlucky? _____.

2. Can you guess what the lucky numbers and the unlucky numbers are in China? Do you know why? _____.

Ex. 1.13 Postcodes. Listen to the recording and write down the postcodes for these 6 cities.

Beijing _____   Shanghai _____

Tianjin _____   Chongqing _____

Lhasa _____   Dunhuang _____

Ex. 1.14 Country/city names. Listen to the pronunciation. Can you work out what countries/cities these are and write their names in English?

1. Xiānggǎng _____   Mǎláixīyà _____   Fēilǜbīn _____

2. Hélán _____   Pútáoyá _____   Ài'ěrlán _____

3. Yīngguó _____   Fǎguó _____   Yìndùníxīyà _____

4. Xīnjiāpō _____   Bǐlìshí _____   Xībānyá _____

5. Yìdàlì _____   Zhōngguó _____   Déguó _____

Unit 1
Welcome 欢迎

Ex. 1.15 Now listen carefully. Can you work out the area codes for the following countries / cities? Write the area codes down.

Country/City Name	Area Code	Country/City Name	Area Code
Xiānggǎng		Àomén	
Mǎláixīyà		Yìndùníxīyà	
Fēilǜbīn		Xīnjiāpō	
Hélán		Bǐlìshí	
Pútáoyá		Xībānyá	
Ài'ěrlán		Yìdàlì	
Yīngguó		Zhōngguó	
Fǎguó		Déguó	

Ex. 1.16 Oral practice.

1. Pair work. Use the above table. One student reads out an area code and another student reads out the corresponding country name. Change your roles after every two countries.

2. In-class practice. The teacher reads out a country name and the students read out the corresponding area code.

Ex. 1.17 The following are some countries' area codes. However, the area codes are shown in Chinese characters. Can you help to figure out their names and area codes in English?

Country Name	Pinyin	Area Code	
Denmark	Dānmài	〇〇四五	
	Yìndù	〇〇九一	
	Níbó'ěr	〇〇九七七	

	Yīlǎng	○○九八	
	Āijí	○○二	
	Tǔ'ěrqí	○○九	
	Bājīsītǎn	○○九二	
	Yīlākè	○○九六四	

Ex. 1.18 More numbers. If 12 reads out as "ten-two (shí'èr)", how do you say the following numbers in Chinese?

10   12   14   15   19   20   36   44   78   99

Ex. 1.19 Character practice. Copy each character 3 times in the boxes provided.

Meaning & sounds	Character			
yī one	一			
èr two	二			
sān three	三			

Unit 1
Welcome 欢迎

sì four	四			
wǔ five	五			
liù six	六			
qī seven	七			
bā eight	八			
jiǔ nine	九			
shí ten	十			

Ex. 1.20 Homework. Can you figure out the meanings of the following characters? Write them down in English.

月 _____	口 _____	家 _____	四 _____
日 _____	子 _____	女 _____	龙 _____
水 _____	儿 _____	龟 _____	八 _____
火 _____	人 _____	牛 _____	六 _____
羊 _____	天 _____	五 _____	十 _____
马 _____	小 _____	七 _____	水牛 _____
山 _____	大 _____	九 _____	火山 _____

Ex. 1.21 Here are some useful emergency numbers in China. Can you tell what they are? Please write them and copy the numbers down.

Ambulance service: 一二〇　　Fire: 一一九

Police: 一一〇　　Transport accident: 一二二

British Embassy in Beijing: 〇〇八六一〇五一九二四〇〇〇

British Consulate-general in Shanghai: 〇〇八六二一六二七九七六五〇

United States Embassy in Beijing: 〇〇八六一八六五三二三八三一

Ex. 1.22 Translate the following telephone numbers into Chinese characters.

1507895	51678259	8795429
2878960	45369788	2546987

Unit 1
Welcome 欢迎

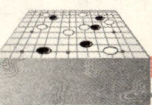

Culture factor

English people believe 13 and 666 are unlucky numbers. China too has lucky and unlucky numbers. For Chinese people the number 3 is lucky. This stems from traditional Taoist beliefs. The numbers 6 and 9 being multiples of 3 are also considered lucky. In China, the number 8 is thought to be lucky as its pronunciation is similar to a word that means "make money (fā)". Similarly, the number 4 is a very unlucky number since it sounds similar to the word for death (sǐ). Due to this, some buildings don't even have a fourth and fourteenth floor, using 3A and 13A instead.

Useful expressions

你好!	Nǐ hǎo!	How do you do! / Hello!
再见!	Zàijiàn!	Goodbye.
谢谢!	Xièxie!	Thank you.
欢迎!	Huānyíng!	Welcome!

Unit 2
Introduce Myself 我是……

In this unit you will learn:

- greetings
- how to introduce yourself
- countries and nationalities
- how to give your phone number

Task 1   你好

你	nǐ	you
好	hǎo	good, fine
我	wǒ	I, me
是	shì	be (am, is, are)
她	tā	she, her
他	tā	he, him

Ex. 2.1   Listen to the recording and figure out the meaning of the text.

你好！我是小水。

你好！我是大中。

她是小水。

他是大中。

Unit 2
Introduce Myself 我是……

Ex. 2.2 Choose the right English meanings to fill in the blanks.

| be (am, is, are) | he, him | I, me | how do you do |
| you | she, her | good, fine | |

1.	Xiǎoshuǐ	小水	a girl's name
2.	Dàzhōng	大中	a boy's name
3.	nǐ	你	
4.	wǒ	我	
5.	tā	她	
6.	tā	他	
7.	shì	是	
8.	hǎo	好	
9.	nǐ hǎo	你好	

Ex. 2.3 Listen to the wordlist and check your answers.

Grammar Notes   Form of verb

Chinese verbs only have one form. For example, 是 (shì) means "am", "is", "are", "was", "were", "will be", and "would have been".

Ex. 2.4 Oral exercises.

1. Read out the following words.

   我   你   好   她   他   是

   我是   你是   他是   她是   你好

2. How do you say these words in Chinese?
   (1) I am   (2) you are   (3) he is   (4) she is

3. How do Chinese people greet each other?

4. Now, please greet the person sitting next to you in Chinese and introduce yourself with your name.

Ex. 2.5 Character practice. Copy each character 4 times in the boxes provided.

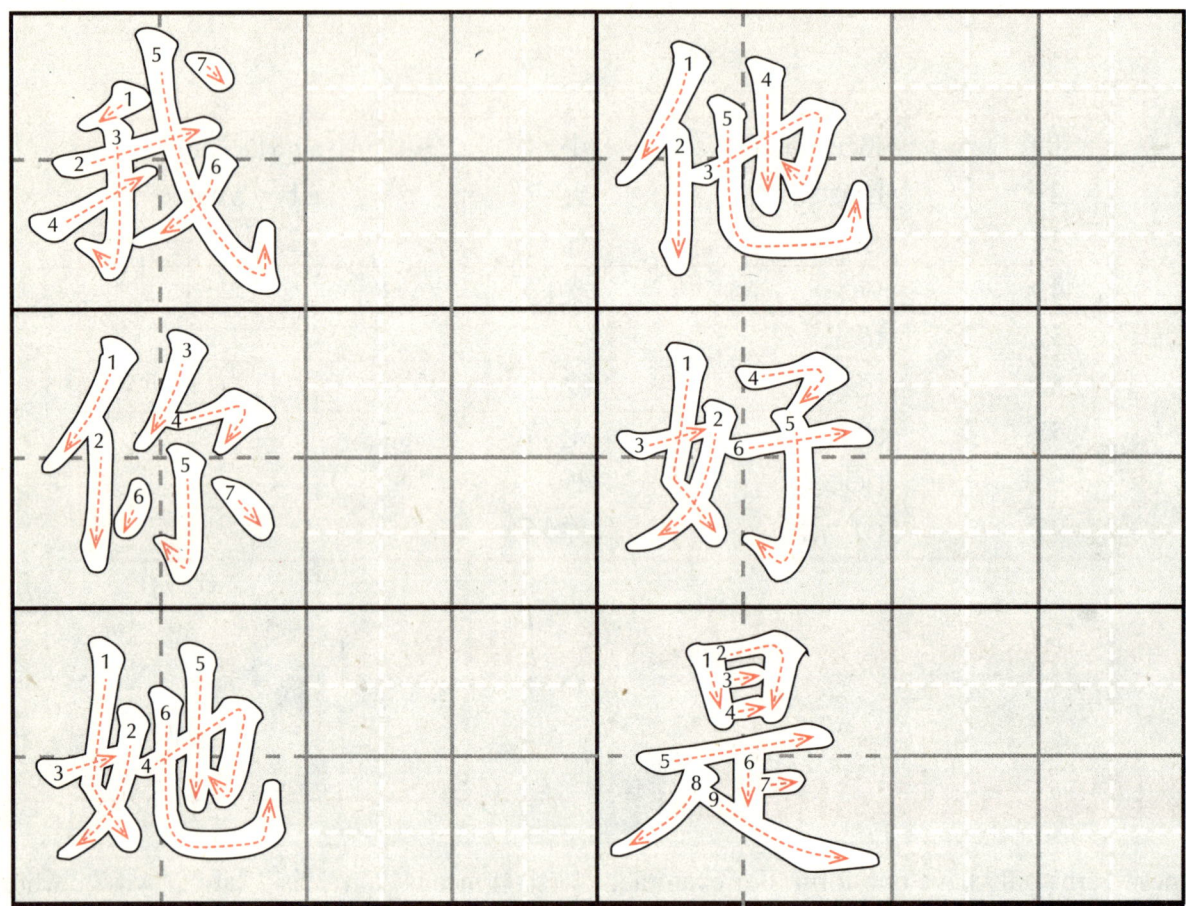

Ex. 2.6 Homework. Translate the following sentences into Chinese.

1. How do you do? I am Big Bull.   _____

2. How do you do? I am Little Moon.   _____

3. She is Little Water.   _____

4. He is Big Hill.   _____

Unit 2
Introduce Myself 我是……

Task 2 我姓王

王	wáng	king; a common surname
姓	xìng	surname
叫	jiào	be called
国	guó	kingdom, state
英	yīng	hero, bravery

Ex. 2.7 Listen to the following introduction carefully.

你好，我姓马，我叫马大中。我是英国人。

你好！我姓王，我叫王小水。我是中国人。

Ex. 2.8 Choose the right English meanings to fill in the blanks.

My surname is Wang.	I am called Xiaoshui.	China
I am British.	I am Dazhong.	United Kingdom
How do you do?	I am called Ma Dazhong.	I am Chinese.
middle, centre	kingdom, state	hero, bravery
surname	king; a common surname	be called

1.	Nǐ hǎo!	你好！	
2.	Wǒ xìng Wáng.	我姓王。	
3.	Wǒ jiào Xiǎoshuǐ.	我叫小水。	
4.	Wǒ jiào Mǎ Dàzhōng.	我叫马大中。	
5.	Wǒ shì Dàzhōng.	我是大中。	
6.	Wǒ shì Yīngguórén.	我是英国人。	

7.	Wǒ shì Zhōngguórén.	我是中国人。	
8.	Yīngguó	英国	
9.	Zhōngguó	中国	
10.	zhōng	中	
11.	guó	国	
12.	yīng	英	
13.	xìng	姓	
14.	jiào	叫	
15.	wáng	王	

Ex. 2.9   Listen to the wordlist and check your answers.

Grammar Notes   Name & Nationality

1. The word 姓 (xìng, surname) can be used as a verb in Chinese, which means "to be surnamed". Here are examples of how to introduce one's surname and given name.

>   My surname is Wang.　　我姓王。
>   I am called Xiaoshui.　　我叫小水。

2. Chinese names are always surname first. If one's surname is 马 (Mǎ) and given name is 大中 (Dàzhōng), he/she can introduce himself/herself in the following ways:

>   I am called Ma Dazhong.　　我叫马大中。　　(full name)
>   I am Ma Dazhong.　　我是马大中。　　(full name)
>   My surname is Ma.　　我姓马。　　(surname)
>   I am called Dazhong.　　我叫大中。　　(given name)

3. Introduce one's nationality, or where one is from, using the pattern 是……人 (shì...rén).

>   I am Chinese.　　我是中国人。
>   You are British.　　你是英国人。
>   He is from Beijing.　　他是Beijing人。

Ex. 2.10   Say the following expressions in Chinese.

I am ... _____　　He is ... _____
I am called ... _____　　His surname is ... _____
How do you do? _____　　She is Xiaoshui. _____
I am English. _____　　You are Chinese. _____

Unit 2
Introduce Myself 我是……

Ex. 2.11 Do you still remember the countries' names you learnt in Unit 1? Since each character has its own meaning, the following countries each have their own literal meanings. Can you match them?

Yīngguó	英国	United Kingdom		the Middle Kingdom
Měiguó	美国	America		the Country of Braveness
Zhōngguó	中国	China		the Country of Beauty
Fǎguó	法国	France		the Country of Morality
Déguó	德国	Germany		the Country of Law

Ex. 2.12 We have learnt 人(rén) in Unit 1. It means "person, people". If British people are 英国人, how do you refer to American, Chinese, French, German people and people from London and Paris?

英国		Yīngguó	英国人 Yīngguórén
美国		Měiguó	
中国		Zhōngguó	
法国		Fǎguó	
德国		Déguó	
London		Lúndūn	
Paris		Bālí	

25

Ex. 2.13 Now, please greet the person sitting next to you and introduce yourself using the following patterns. Ask your teacher how to pronounce your city's name in Chinese.

你好！我是_____。

我姓_____，我叫_____。

我是_____国人。我是_____（your city）人。

Ex. 2.14 Character practice. Copy each character 4 times in the boxes provided.

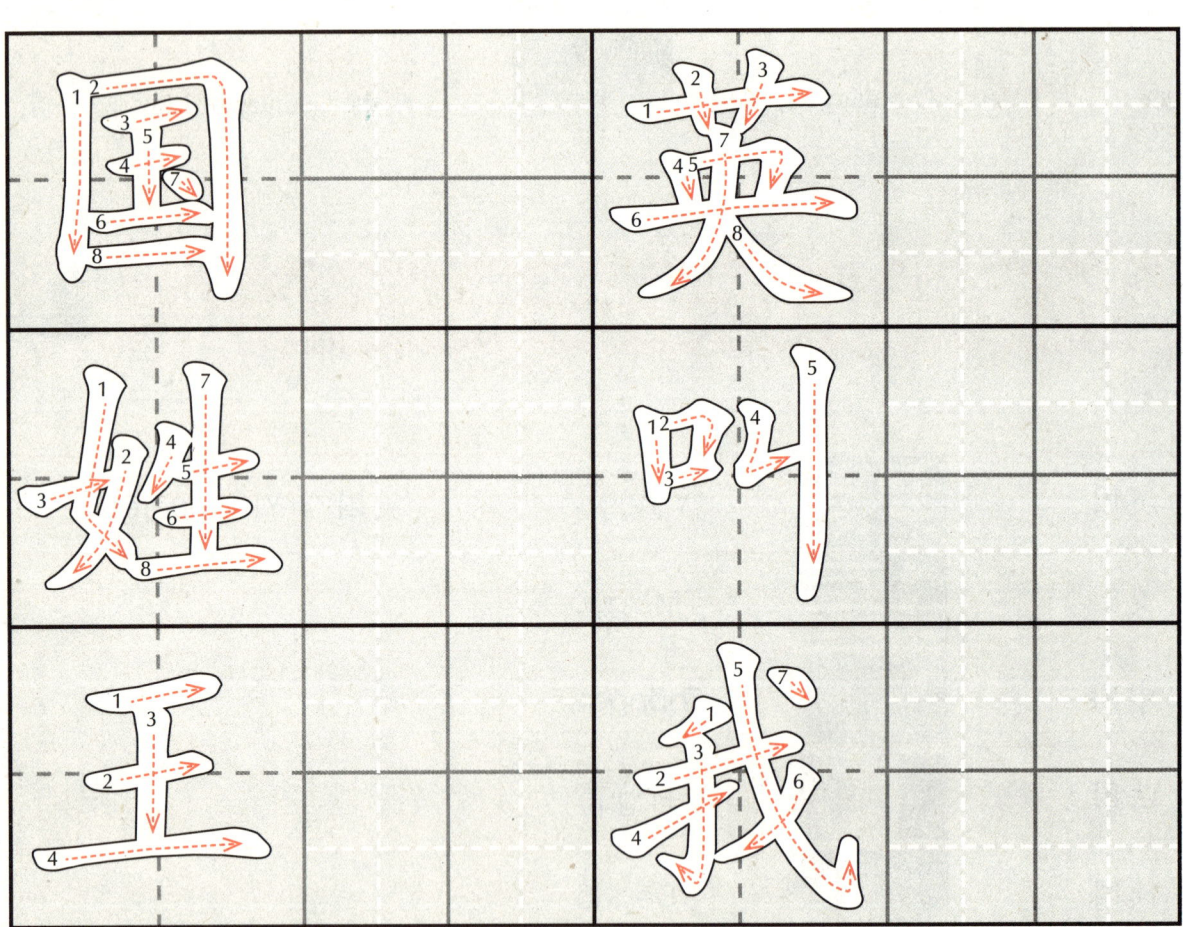

Unit 2
Introduce Myself 我是……

Ex. 2.15   Homework.

1. Your friend is British. Can you describe his nationality in Chinese? Write down your sentence in the boxes provided.

2. We know 王 (wáng) means "king". It is also a popular surname in Chinese. Can you guess the meanings of the following words?

　　　王家　　　　小王　　　　　国王　　　　王国

　　　女王　　　　王子　　　　　英国女王

Task 3   我的电话是……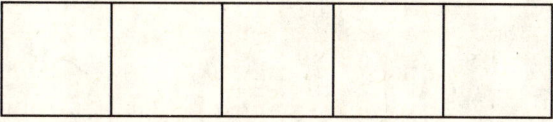

美	měi	beautiful
们	men	plural marker
的	de	possessive particle
电	diàn	electricity, tele-
话	huà	speech, sayings, language

Ex. 2.16   Listen to the recording carefully.

(Ring… Ring… Hi, it's 大牛 here. I am not in at the moment. Please leave your name and telephone number after the beep. I will get back to you as soon as possible. BEEEEP…)

你好！大牛。我是马大中。我是马小美。

我们的电话是020 3746 5289。

Ex. 2.17 Choose the right English meanings to fill in the blanks.

telephone	possessive particle	ours	
we, us	a surname; king	beautiful	
bull	horse	middle	
electricity, tele-	speech, sayings, language	plural marker	

1.	men	们	
2.	wǒmen	我们	
3.	de	的	
4.	wǒmen de	我们的	
5.	diàn	电	
6.	huà	话	
7.	diànhuà	电话	
8.	wáng	王	
9.	zhōng	中	
10.	niú	牛	
11.	mǎ	马	
12.	měi	美	

Ex. 2.18 Listen to the wordlist and check your answers.

Grammar Notes — Plural marker & possessive marker

1. Generally speaking, there is no difference between the single form and the plural form in Chinese. An exception to this is that after pronouns and certain nouns, 们 (men) is used as a suffix to give plural meanings.

2. 的 (de) is the possessive marker. 我的 (wǒ de) means "my", 大中的 (Dàzhōng de) means "Dazhong's".

3. There is no case in Chinese. For example, 我 (wǒ) indicates both "I" and "me". 他 (tā) indicates both "he" and "him".

28

Unit 2
Introduce Myself 我是……

Ex. 2.19 How do you express the following plural forms? Choose the correct characters to fill in the blanks.

> 你　我　她　他　他们　她们　我们　你们

I, me _____   we, us _____
you _____   you (plural) _____
he, him _____   they, them (male) _____
she, her _____   they, them (female) _____

Ex. 2.20 的 is a marker to show possession. Can you finish the following tasks by writing their possession forms?

我 ⇒ _____ (my)   我们 ⇒ _____ (ours)
你 ⇒ _____ (your)   你们 ⇒ _____ (yours)
他 ⇒ _____ (his)   他们 ⇒ _____ (their)
她 ⇒ _____ (her)   大中 ⇒ _____ (Dazhong's)

Ex. 2.21 Pair work.

Two of you have 小美的电话 book (Card A) and 大中的电话 book (Card B) respectively. Can you exchange information so as to complete your books? Use the following pattern:

"一"是大牛。大牛是中国人，他的电话是_____。
"二"是……

Card A　小美的电话 book

1.	大牛	Chinese	0086-10-7895 4261
2.	小水		
3.	Stephanie	French	0033-1-5896 425
4.	小英		
5.	Peter	German	003-49-895 672
6.	Sarah		
7.	小王	Beijingese	0086-10-7895 6468
8.	小好		

Card B 大中的电话book

1. 大牛		
2. 小水	American	001-389-4586 365
3. Stephanie		
4. 小英	Hongkongese	00852-3458 0028
5. Peter		
6. Sarah	English	44-078-9265 678
7. 小王		
8. 小好	Shanghainese	0086-20-1364 5898

Ex. 2.22 Character practice. Copy each character 4 times in the boxes provided.

们			的		
电			话		
美			国		

30

Unit 2
Introduce Myself 我是……

Ex. 2.23　Homework.

1. Can you write a sentence to introduce yourself in Chinese? Here is an example.

    你好！我是小美，我是中国人，我的电话是0086108945632。

    Your sentence:_____

2. Read aloud the following words and say their meanings.

    英国　　英国人　　美国　　美国人　　美人

    中国　　电话　　　好人　　好电话　　我的电话

3. Translate the following sentences into Chinese.

    (1) We are British.

    (2) She is Chinese.

    (3) They are American.

    (4) His telephone is mine.

    (5) My telephone number is 0798 6784 2351.

Culture factor

Much like in Britain there are common and rare surnames in China. There are about 500 surnames that are all recorded in a book called *Bai Jia Xing* (百家姓, Book of a Hundred Surnames), which was compiled under China's Song Dynasty in the 10th century. By far the most common surnames in China are Li, Wang and Zhang, but the surnames Chen, Zhu, Lin, Hu, Sun, Zhao and Gao are also very common.

Useful expressions

早!	Zǎo!	Morning.
早上好!	Zǎoshang hǎo!	Good morning.
下午好!	Xiàwǔ hǎo!	Good afternoon.
晚上好!	Wǎnshang hǎo!	Good evening.
不用谢!	Bú yòng xiè!	You are welcome!

Unit 3
My Family 我的家人

In this unit you will learn:
- about family members
- about pets
- how to ask different types of questions

Task 1 他们是我的家人

爸	bà	father
妈	mā	mother
弟	dì	younger brother
这	zhè/zhèi	this
那	nà/nèi	that

Ex. 3.1 Look at the picture of a family and listen to the recording.

他们是我的家人。 他是我爸爸。那是我妈妈。

这是我。 那是我弟弟。

Ex. 3.2 Choose the right English meanings to fill in the blanks.

mother	younger brother	this	I, me
father	family members	that	home, family

1.	jiā	家	
2.	jiārén	家人	
3.	zhè/zhèi	这	
4.	nà/nèi	那	
5.	bàba	爸爸	
6.	māma	妈妈	
7.	wǒ	我	
8.	dìdi	弟弟	

Ex. 3.3 Listen to the wordlist and check your answers.

Ex. 3.4 Extra vocabulary. Here are more relatives. Can you guess their meanings? Choose the correct words to fill in the blanks.

father	mother	elder brother	younger brother
grandmother	grandfather	younger sister	I, me

	我		
	爸爸		
jiějie	姐姐	elder sister	
gēge	哥哥		
	妈妈		
mèimei	妹妹		
yéye	爷爷		
nǎinai	奶奶		
	弟弟		

Remember, characters with 父 relate to male, and those with 女 link to female.

Ex. 3.5 Listen to the extra vocabulary and check your answers.

Unit 3
My Family 我的家人

Ex. 3.6 Can you introduce the members of these two families to your classmates and teacher?

大龙的家人

小好的家人

Ex. 3.7 Character practice. Copy each character 4 times in the boxes provided.

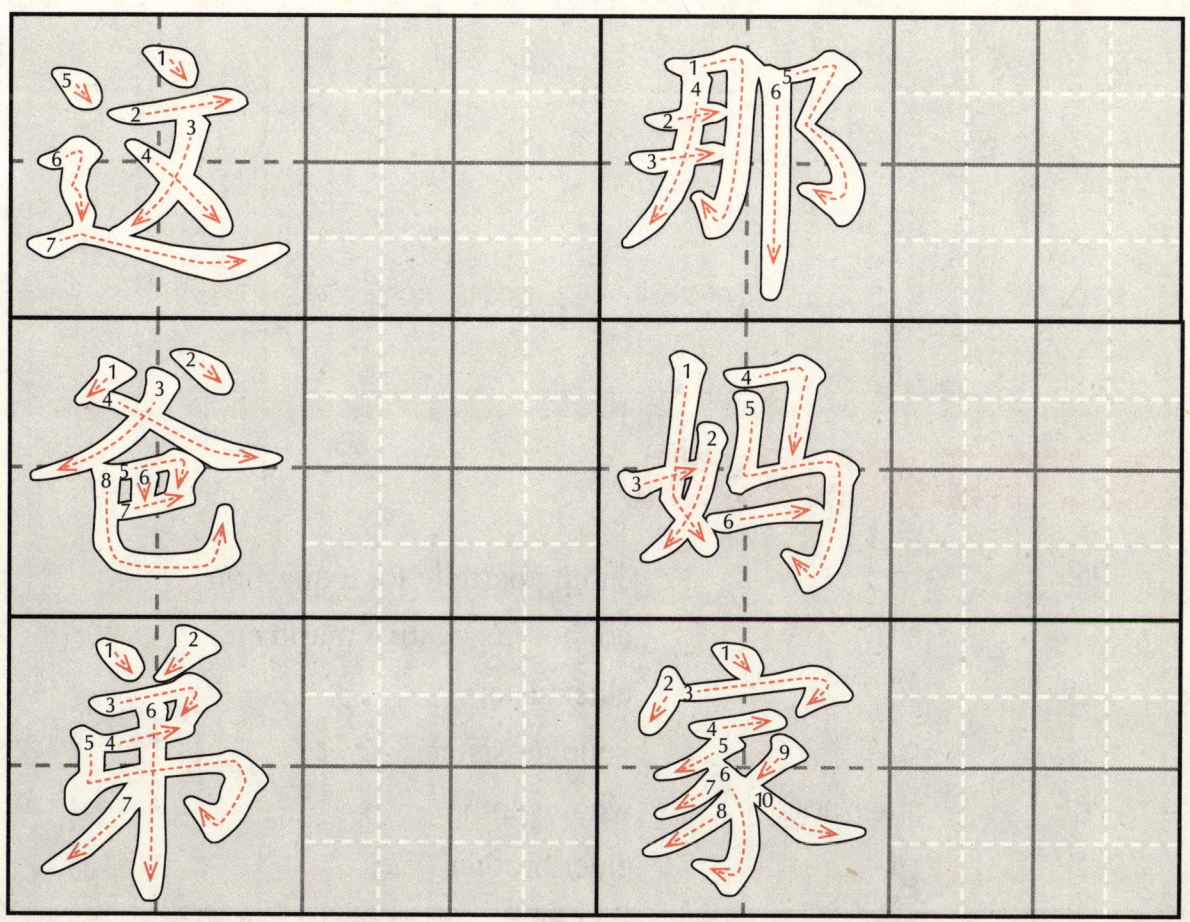

Ex. 3.8   Homework.

1. Here is your friend 小马 and her family. Can you introduce them in Chinese?

2. Find a photo of your family or draw one, and write down your introduction in Chinese.

Task 2   她不是我妹妹

吗	ma	ending particle for a question
不	bù	no, not (a negative marker)
姐	jiě	elder sister
妹	mèi	younger sister
谁	shéi/shuí	who, whom
哥	gē	elder brother

Unit 3
My Family 我的家人

Ex. 3.9 Listen to the following dialogue carefully.

A：她是你姐姐吗？

B：她不是我姐姐。

A：她是你妹妹吗？

B：她不是我妹妹。

A：她是谁？

B：她是小美，是大中的妹妹。大中是她的哥哥。

Ex. 3.10 Choose the right English meanings to fill in the blanks.

elder brother	ending particle for a question	who, whom
younger sister	elder sister	no, not
be (am, is, are)	am/is/are not	

1.	ma	吗	
2.	bù	不	
3.	shì	是	
4.	bú shì	不是	
5.	shéi/shuí	谁	
6.	gēge	哥哥	
7.	jiějie	姐姐	
8.	mèimei	妹妹	

Ex. 3.11 Listen to the wordlist and check your answers.

Grammar Notes Negative marker & question marker

1. 不(bù) is a negative marker. It is always used before a verb, it means "not".

   ▶ 小水不是中国人,她是英国人。

2. 吗(ma) is used to make a sentence into a general question. Use 吗 to ask a question if you want to know whether 小水(Xiǎoshuǐ) is English.

   ▶ 小水是英国人吗?

3. 谁(shéi/shuí) means "who" and "whom". It is used to ask a specific question. For example, use 谁 to replace 小水 to create a question if you have no idea who is English.

   ▶ 谁是英国人?

Ex. 3.12 Add 不 into the sentences and change them into negative forms.

Here is an example: 我是中国人。 → 我不是中国人。

1. 我姓王。	2. 他叫马大山。	3. 这是我哥哥。
4. 他是我爸爸。	5. 那是我妈妈。	6. 这是中国。

Unit 3
My Family 我的家人

Ex. 3.13 Read out the following sentences. Pay attention to the questions with 吗.

1. 你是中国人。	你是中国人吗？
2. 他是英国人。	他是英国人吗？
3. 她姓王。	她姓王吗？
4. 这是他弟弟。	这是他弟弟吗？
5. 那是她妈妈。	那是她妈妈吗？

Ex. 3.14 Please match 谁(shéi/shuí) questions with their meanings.

谁是英国人？	Who is he?
她是谁？	Who is she?
谁是小英的妈妈？	Who is Xiaoying's mother?
谁是中国人？	Who is his father?
谁是他的爸爸？	Who is Chinese?
他是谁？	Who is English?

Ex. 3.15 Character practice. Copy each character 4 times in the boxes provided.

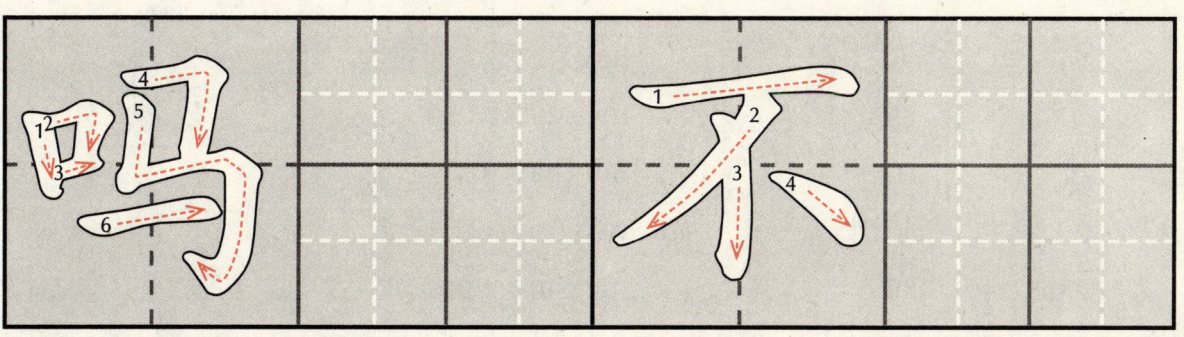

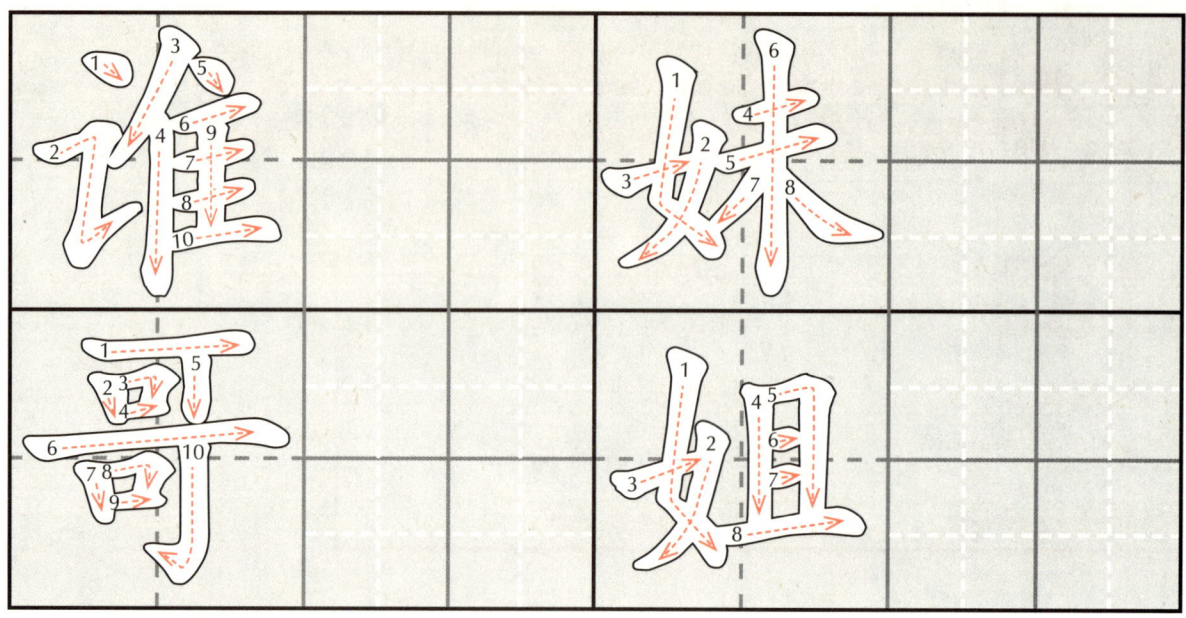

Ex. 3.16   Homework. Translate the following sentences into Chinese.

1. I am called Xiaoshui.
2. A: Are you Xiaoying? B: No, I am not.
3. A: Is your surname Wang? B: Yes.
4. He is Chinese.
5. My father is not Chinese.
6. A: Are you Chinese? B: Yes, I am.
7. Who is Chinese?
8. Who is not Chinese?
9. Who is your younger sister?
10. Who is Xiaoying's elder brother?

Task 3   我家有两只狗

有	yǒu	have
个	gè	measure word
没	méi	not (have)
两	liǎng	two (of)
只	zhī	measure word
狗	gǒu	dog

Unit 3
My Family 我的家人

Ex. 3.17 Listen to the recording carefully.

你们好！我叫美英。我家有五口人。爸爸，妈妈，我，一个妹妹，一个弟弟。我没有哥哥，没有姐姐。

我家有两只狗，一只大狗，一只小狗。大狗是美国狗，小狗是中国狗。我们没有英国狗。你家有没有狗？

Ex. 3.18 Choose the right English meanings to fill in the blanks.

have	not have	do (you) have…?	
two (of)	an elder sister	five family members	
dog	big dog	two dogs	negative marker for 有

1.	kǒu	口	mouth; a measure word
2.	wǔ kǒu rén	五口人	
3.	gè	个	individual; a common measure word
4.	yí gè jiějie	一个姐姐	
5.	zhī	只	single; a measure word for small animals
6.	liǎng zhī gǒu	两只狗	
7.	liǎng	两	
8.	gǒu	狗	
9.	dà gǒu	大狗	
10.	yǒu	有	
11.	méi	没	
12.	méiyǒu	没有	
13.	yǒu méiyǒu	有没有	

41

Ex. 3.19 Listen to the wordlist and check your answers.

Grammar Notes   Choice type questions

1. Apart from putting 吗(ma) at the end of a sentence to ask question, another popular way to ask question is to make "Yes or No" questions. Simply put the positive form and the negative form of the verbs together.

2. 有(yǒu) means "to have". The negative form for 有 is always 没有(méiyǒu)。The negative form for 是(shì) is always 不是(bú shì).

   是+不是   >>>>   她是不是中国人?
                    这是不是你的狗?
                    那是不是你弟弟?

   有+没有   >>>>   你有没有妹妹?
                    他有没有狗?
                    爸爸有没有电话?

Ex. 3.20 Read aloud the following sentences.

他有妹妹。   你是英国人。
他没有妹妹。   你不是英国人。
他有没有妹妹?   你是不是英国人?
他有妹妹吗?   你是英国人吗?
谁有妹妹?   谁是英国人?

Unit 3
My Family 我的家人

Grammar Notes 的 & measure word

1. Possessive marker 的 (de) is optional when refers to one's family.

> 我家   你家   他家   他们家   小英家   大中家

2. Chinese has a special system called measure words to categorise nouns. Measure words are used before nouns to show their categories. Measure words are always used after numbers and 这/那 before a noun.

> 五个人 (wǔ gè rén) five men
> 这只狗 (zhè zhī gǒu) this dog
> 那三个英国人 (nà sān gè Yīngguórén) those three Englishmen

3. There are about 20 frequently used measure words in Chinese, you have been introduced to three of them in this task.

> 个 (gè) is the most common measure word in Chinese.
> 口 (kǒu) means mouth, and is used to describe how many people there are in a family.
> 只 (zhī) is used for a small animal.

4. 两 (liǎng) means "two of something". Numbers like twelve and twenty-two, use 二 (èr).

> 两个人   十二个人
> 两只狗   二十二只狗

Ex. 3.21 Can you figure out the measure words for the following sentences?

1. 我家有五____人。

2. 他有一____姐姐，没有妹妹。

3. 我妈妈有一____电话。

4. 这____英国狗大。

5. 那____中国人有两____狗。

Grammar Notes   Adjective sentence

1. 美，大，小 are adjectives. Adjectives can be used as verbs in Chinese. The negative marker for an adjective is 不(bù). Please note the verb "is" is omitted in the following sentences:

   She is not pretty.   她不美。
   The United Kingdom is small, and the United States is big.   英国小，美国大。
   My dog is big, and my brother's dog is small.   我的狗大，哥哥的狗小。
   This English man is good, and those two Englishmen are not good.
   这个英国人好，那两个英国人不好。

3. Choice type questions and 吗(ma) questions for adjective sentence are:

   Is your dog big?   你的狗大不大?
                               你的狗大吗?

   Is his phone good?   他的电话好不好?
                               他的电话好吗?

Ex. 3.22   Read aloud the following sentences and then translate them into English.

1. 这个人好, 那个人不好。 _____

2. 这个电话好, 那个电话不好。 _____

3. 这只狗大, 那只狗不大。 _____

4. 英国狗大, 中国狗不大。 _____

5. 哥哥的狗大, 我的狗小。 _____

Unit 3
My Family 我的家人

Ex. 3.23 Character practice. Copy each character 4 times in the boxes provided.

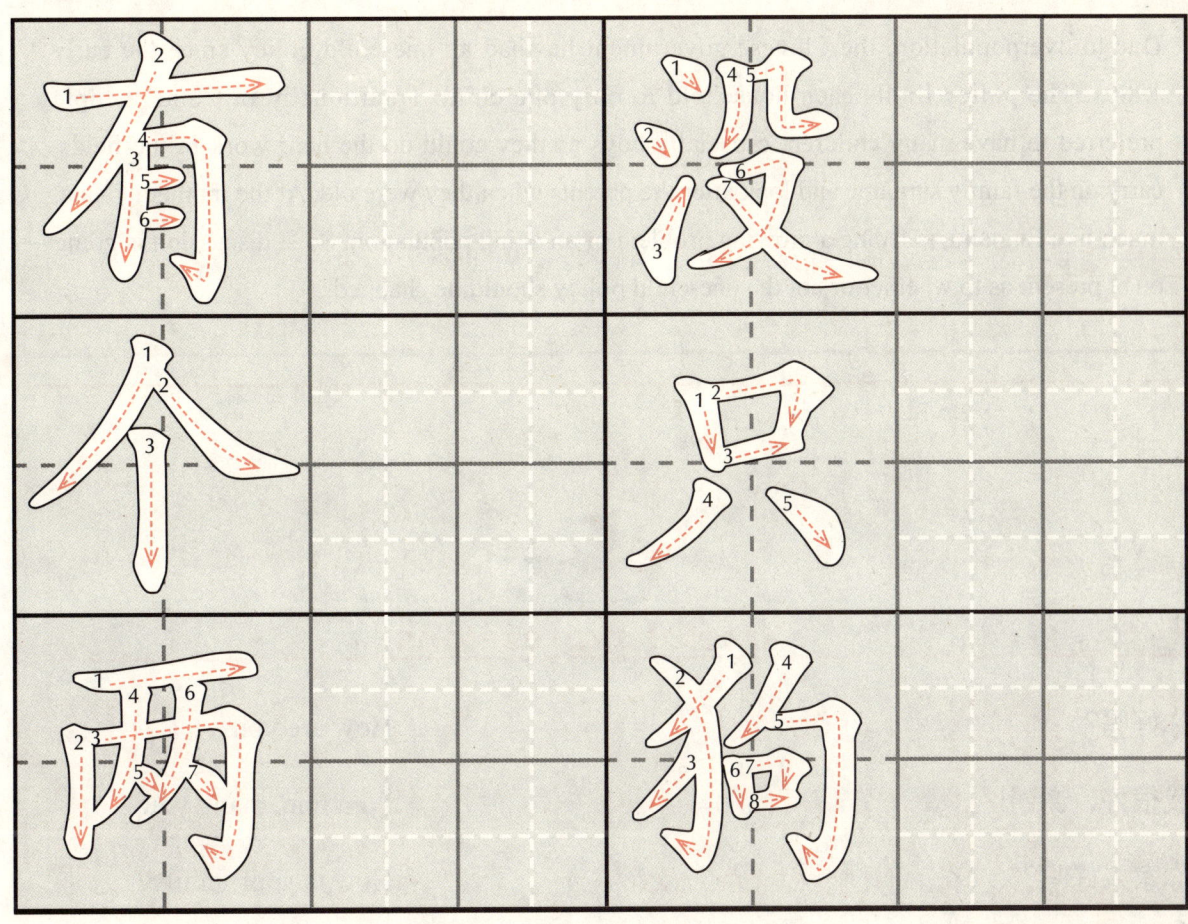

Ex. 3.24 Homework. Translate the following sentences into Chinese.

1. I have an elder sister. _____

2. My mum doesn't have a younger brother, but a younger sister.

   _____

3. These two English dogs are big. _____

4. Does your younger sister have a dog? _____

5. My father has two telephones, one is good, and the other one is not good.

   _____

Culture factor

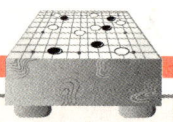

Due to overpopulation, the Chinese government has had an one-child policy since the early 1980s. The policy limits each household to only one child. Traditionally in China, people preferred to have many children, especially boys as they could do the hard work in the fields, carry on the family surname and look after the parents when they were old. At the moment China, much like England, is facing a growing problem of an aging population. So, a discussion is going on at present as to whether or not the one-child policy should be changed.

Useful expressions

你好吗？	Nǐ hǎo ma?	How are you?
我很好，谢谢！	Wǒ hěn hǎo, xièxie!	I am fine, thank you.
你家人好吗？	Nǐ jiārén hǎo ma?	How is your family?
很好，谢谢。	Hěn hǎo, xièxie.	(They are) Fine, thanks.

Unit 4

The Family 家人

In this unit you will learn:
- how to give information about yourself and your family
- likes and dislikes
- how to ask specific questions with question words

Task 1 你叫什么?

什	shén	what
么	me	a particle used in 什么 (what)
哪	nǎ	which
呢	ne	ending particle for a question marker
几	jǐ	how many/much

Ex. 4.1 Listen to the following dialogue carefully.

王大山: 你好!
娜 娜: 你好!
王大山: 我姓王,叫王大山。你姓什么? 叫什么?
娜 娜: 我姓White, 叫Nana。
王大山: 我是中国人。你呢?
娜 娜: 我是英国人。你家有几口人?

王大山：我家有三口人，爸爸，妈妈，我。你家呢？

娜　娜：我家有五口人，我爸爸，妈妈，我，一个姐姐，一个弟弟。

Ex. 4.2　Choose the right English meanings to fill in the blanks.

United Kingdom　　　which country　　　people from which country
what　　　　　　　　how about…?　　　how about your family
how many family members　　　　　　how many/much
which　　　　　　　where

1.	ne	呢	
2.	nǐ jiā ne	你家呢	
3.	shénme	什么	
4.	nǎ	哪	
5.	nǎr	哪儿	
6.	nǎ guó	哪国	
7.	nǎ guó rén	哪国人	
8.	Yīngguó	英国	
9.	jǐ	几	
10.	jǐ kǒu rén	几口人	

Ex. 4.3　Listen to the wordlist and check your answers.

Ex. 4.4　Based on what you have just heard, answer the following questions in Chinese.

1. What's the surname and given name of the girl?
2. What's the surname and given name of the boy?
3. How many family members does the girl have? Who are they?
4. How many family members does the boy have? Who are they?

Unit 4
The Family 家人

Grammar Notes 呢

呢(ne) is a common sentence ending marker for a question sentence. It means "how about" and indicates a follow up question.

    I am English, how about you?   我是英国人, 你呢?

    I have a dog, how about you?   我有一只狗, 你呢?

Ex. 4.5 Answer the following 呢 questions in Chinese.

1. 我是中国人, 你呢?
2. 我姓王, 你呢?
3. 我叫小美, 你呢?
4. 我有两个妹妹, 你呢?
5. 他没有狗, 你呢?
6. 我家有四口人, 你家呢?
7. 这个电话是你的, 那个呢?

Grammar Notes 这儿, 那儿 & 哪儿

1. You may find 那(nà), 这(zhè) and 哪(nǎ) very useful. Simply add a suffix 儿(-r), and then you will have 那儿(nàr), 这儿(zhèr), and 哪儿(nǎr).

    this   这   here   这儿
    that   那   there   那儿
    which 哪   where 哪儿

2. We have learnt 谁(shéi/shuí, who/whom) in the previous lesson. Here are some more specific question words.

    who/whom 谁   where 哪儿   which country 哪国
    how many/much (for small numbers) 几   what 什么

Ex. 4.6 Can you figure out the meanings of the words in colour?

例： 谁是你弟弟？　　　　　（who/whom）
　　 你是哪国人？　　　　　（　　　　　）
　　 你是中国哪儿人？　　　（　　　　　）
　　 你姓什么？　　　　　　（　　　　　）
　　 你家有几口人？　　　　（　　　　　）

Ex. 4.7 Pair work. Ask and answer the following questions in Chinese.

1. What's your nationality?
2. What's your name?
3. How many people are there in your family?
4. Do you have any younger sisters?
5. How many elder sisters do you have?
6. What's your younger brother's name?
7. What's your elder brother's name?
8. Do you have a dog?
9. How many dogs do you have?
10. Do you have a phone?

Ex. 4.8 Listening exercise. Listen to the following interviews and circle the correct answers.

A. 中国人　　　B. 英国人　　　C. 美国人

A. 爸爸　　　　B. 爸爸的哥哥　　C. 我弟弟

A. 三口人　　　B. 两口人　　　　C. 四口人

Unit 4
The Family 家人

Ex. 4.9 Character practice. Copy each character 4 times in the boxes provided.

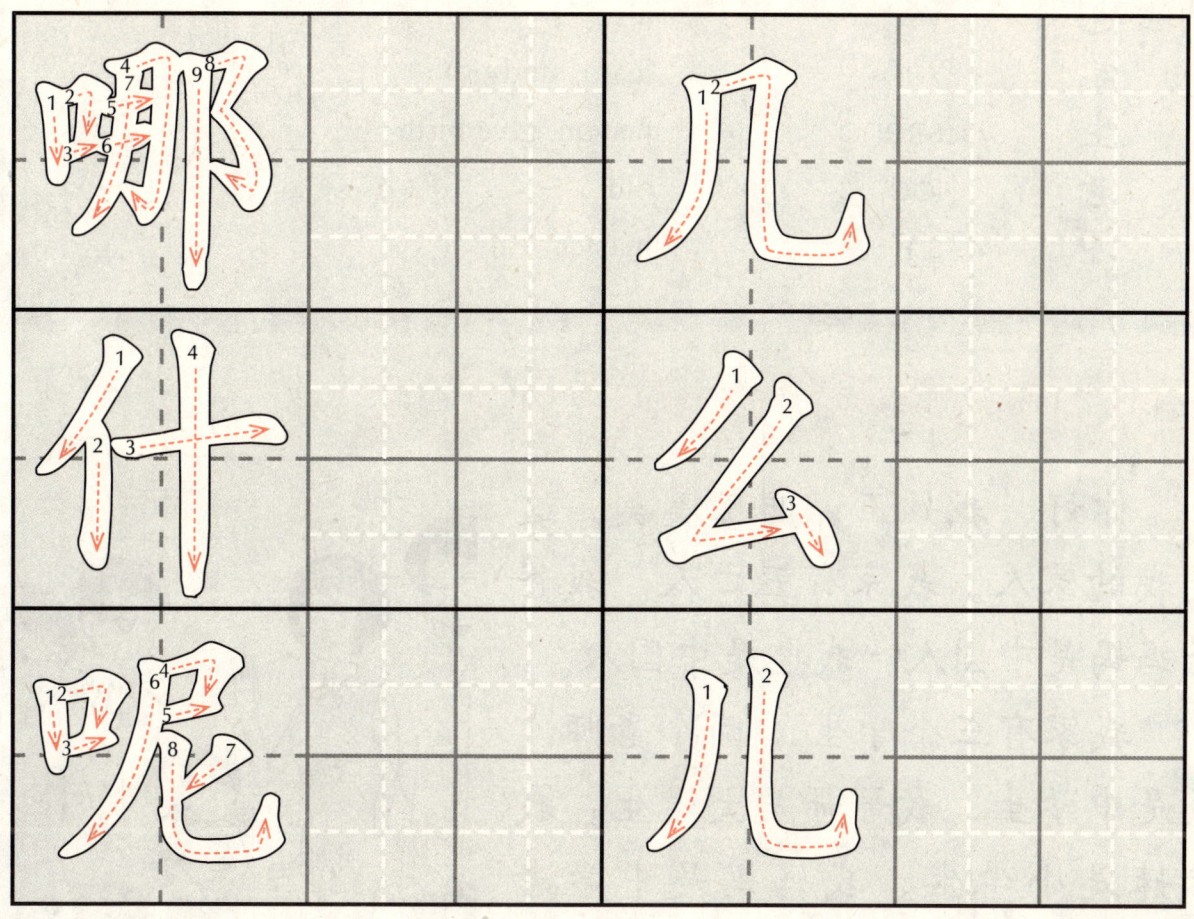

Ex. 4.10 Homework. Make question sentences using the words provided in the brackets.

1. 他是中国人。　　　　　　　　　(谁) _____
2. 小水的妈妈是英国人。　　　　　(哪) _____
3. 小水的爸爸是中国Beijing人。　(哪儿) _____
4. 哥哥有两只狗。　　　　　　　　(几) _____
5. 他家有六口人。　　　　　　　　(几) _____
6. 我姓王,我叫王小牛。　　　　　(什么) _____
7. 你是英国人。　　　　　　　　　(吗) _____
8. 我没有弟弟。　　　　　　　　　(呢) _____

Task 2   我妈妈是老师

也	yě	also
学	xué	learn, study
生	shēng	person; give birth
老	lǎo	old
师	shī	master

Ex. 4.11   Listen to the recording carefully.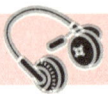

你好，我姓王，叫王美美。这是我的家人。我家有五口人。我爸爸妈妈是中国人，我也是中国人。

我家有三个学生，两个老师。我是中学生，我哥哥是大学生，我妹妹是小学生。我妈妈是中学老师，我爸爸也是老师。他不是中学老师，是大学老师。

Ex. 4.12   Choose the right English meanings to fill in the blanks.

student	primary school	primary school student	teacher
old	university	university student	also
university teacher		secondary school	learn, study
secondary school student		secondary school teacher	

1.	yě	也	
2.	xué	学	
3.	shēng	生	person; give birth
4.	xuésheng	学生	
5.	lǎo	老	

Unit 4
The Family 家人

6.	shī	师	master
7.	lǎoshī	老师	
8.	xiǎoxué	小学	
9.	xiǎoxuéshēng	小学生	
10.	zhōngxué	中学	
11.	zhōngxuéshēng	中学生	
12.	dàxué	大学	
13.	dàxuéshēng	大学生	
14.	zhōngxué lǎoshī	中学老师	
15.	dàxué lǎoshī	大学老师	

Ex. 4.13 Listen to the wordlist and check your answers.

Ex. 4.14 Read the text again and choose whether the following statements are true (✓) or false (✗).

1. Her surname is Xiaomei.   (   )

2. There are four people in her family.   (   )

3. She has an older brother, and he is a university student.   (   )

4. She has an older sister who is a middle school student.   (   )

5. Her mother is a middle school teacher.   (   )

6. Her father is also a teacher at middle school.   (   )

Grammar Notes 也

也 (yě) means "also", and is always used preceding a verb or an adjective. Please note, the verb or the adjective after 也 cannot be omitted.

> 你是中学生，我也。　　　　　✗
> 你是中学生，我也是。　　　　✓
> 你不是大学生，我也不是。　　✓

Ex. 4.15 Find right places in the sentences to insert 也.

1. 爸爸的电话很好。
2. 她不是大学生。
3. 谁有哥哥？
4. 我的老师是美国人。
5. 他家有四口人。

Ex. 4.16 Pair work. Choose 5 questions from below to ask your classmate. Ask and answer in turns.

1. 你姓什么?你叫什么?
2. 你家有几口人?
3. 你是哪国人?
4. 你的电话是什么?
5. 你有没有哥哥/ 姐姐/ 弟弟/ 妹妹? (choose one)
6. 你有几个哥哥/ 姐姐/ 弟弟/ 妹妹? (choose one)
7. 你是不是大学生?
8. 你哥哥是不是大学生?
9. 你有没有狗?你有几只狗?
10. 你的狗是不是英国狗?
11. 你妈妈是不是老师?
12. 你家谁是中学生?

Unit 4
The Family 家人

Ex. 4.17 Character practice. Copy each character 4 times in the boxes provided.

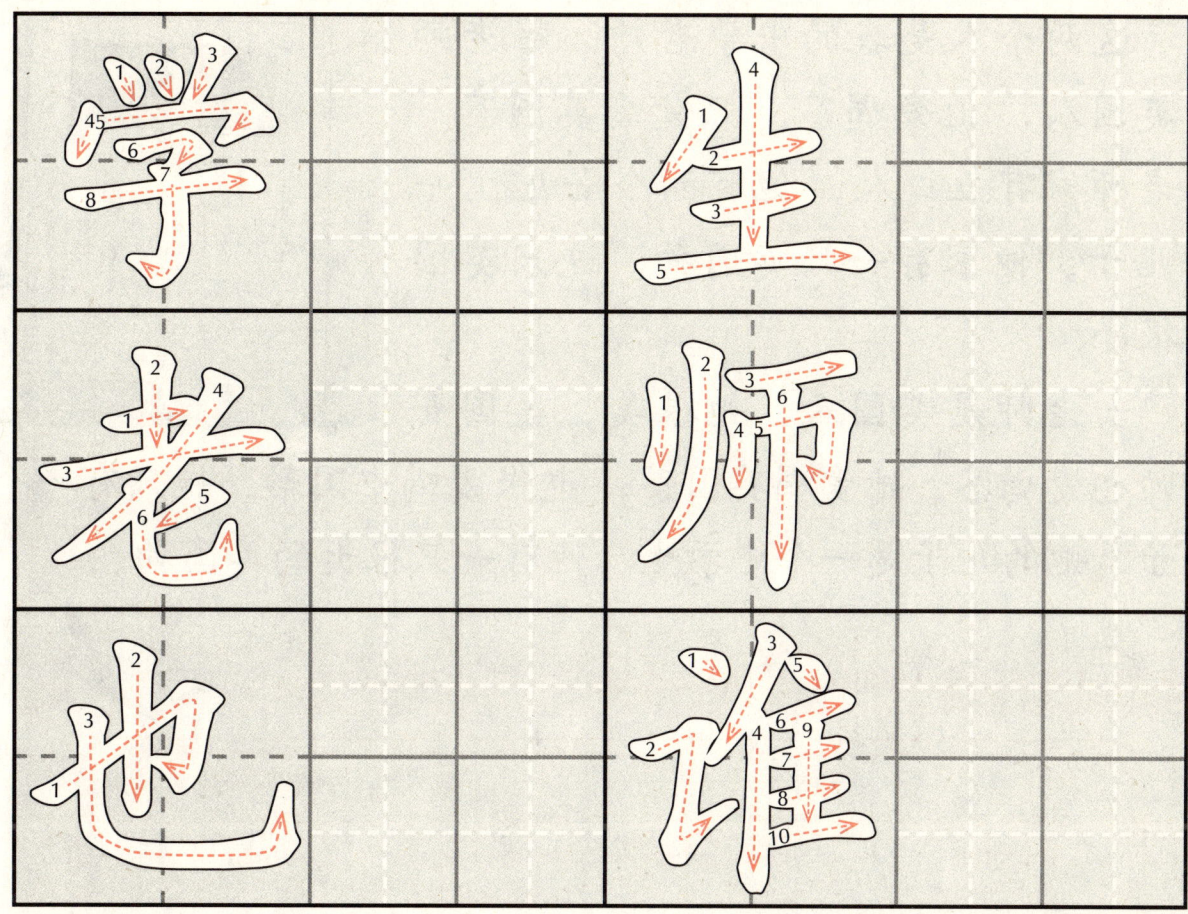

Ex. 4.18 Homework. Copy Ex. 4.16 questions 1-4, 9 & 12, and write down your answers in Chinese.

Task 3   男老师很爱喝英国茶

男	nán	male
爱	ài	love; love to
喝	hē	drink
茶	chá	tea
很	hěn	very

Ex. 4.19 Listen to the recording carefully.

这两个人是我的中学老师。男老师是英国人，他爱喝茶，只爱喝英国茶。男老师家有五口人，他有两个女儿，一个儿子。他家有一只英国狗。这只英国狗很小。

女老师是美国人，她很美。美国女老师也爱喝茶，她爱喝英国茶，也很爱喝中国茶。她只有一个儿子，她的儿子是一个中学生。他有一只很大的美国狗。

Ex. 4.20 Choose the right English meanings to fill in the blanks.

only	very	tea	love; love to
drink	male	female	son
daughter	male teacher	female teacher	woman
girl student	man	boy student	

1.	nán	男	
2.	nǚ	女	
3.	nán lǎoshī	男老师	
4.	nǚ lǎoshī	女老师	
5.	érzi	儿子	
6.	nǚ'ér	女儿	
7.	hěn	很	
8.	zhǐ	只	
9.	hē	喝	
10.	ài	爱	
11.	chá	茶	
12.	nánrén	男人	
13.	nǚrén	女人	
14.	nán xuésheng	男学生	
15.	nǚ xuésheng	女学生	

Unit 4
The Family 家人

Ex. 4.21 Listen to the wordlist and check your answers.

Ex. 4.22 Read the text again. And answer the following questions in Chinese.

1. Who are these two people?

2. Who loves to drink only English tea?

3. Who loves to drink Chinese Tea?

4. How many people are there in the male teacher's family? Does he have a daughter?

5. Does the female teacher have a daughter?

6. Who has a British dog? Who has an American dog?

Grammar Notes   Two adverbs 很 & 只

1. 很 (hěn) means "very".

    很大   很好   很爱喝茶

    Note: 的 (de) must be used when "很 + Adj." precedes a noun.

    狗   茶   人
    大狗   好茶   好人
    很大的狗   很好的茶   很好的人

2. 只 (zhǐ) is used as an adverb here. It means "only, just".

    我家只有三口人。
    我不是大学生,我只是一个中学生。

    Note: It shares the written form of measure word 只 (zhī), but with different tones and meanings.

    她只有一个儿子。 VS 她儿子有一只大狗。

Ex. 4.23 Read aloud the following build-up sentences.

茶
中国茶
喝中国茶
很爱喝中国茶
老师很爱喝中国茶。
女老师很爱喝中国茶。
英国女老师很爱喝中国茶。

狗
大狗
一只大狗
有一只大狗
只有一只大狗
弟弟只有一只大狗。
大中的弟弟只有一只大狗。

Ex. 4.24 Character practice. Copy each character 4 times in the boxes provided.

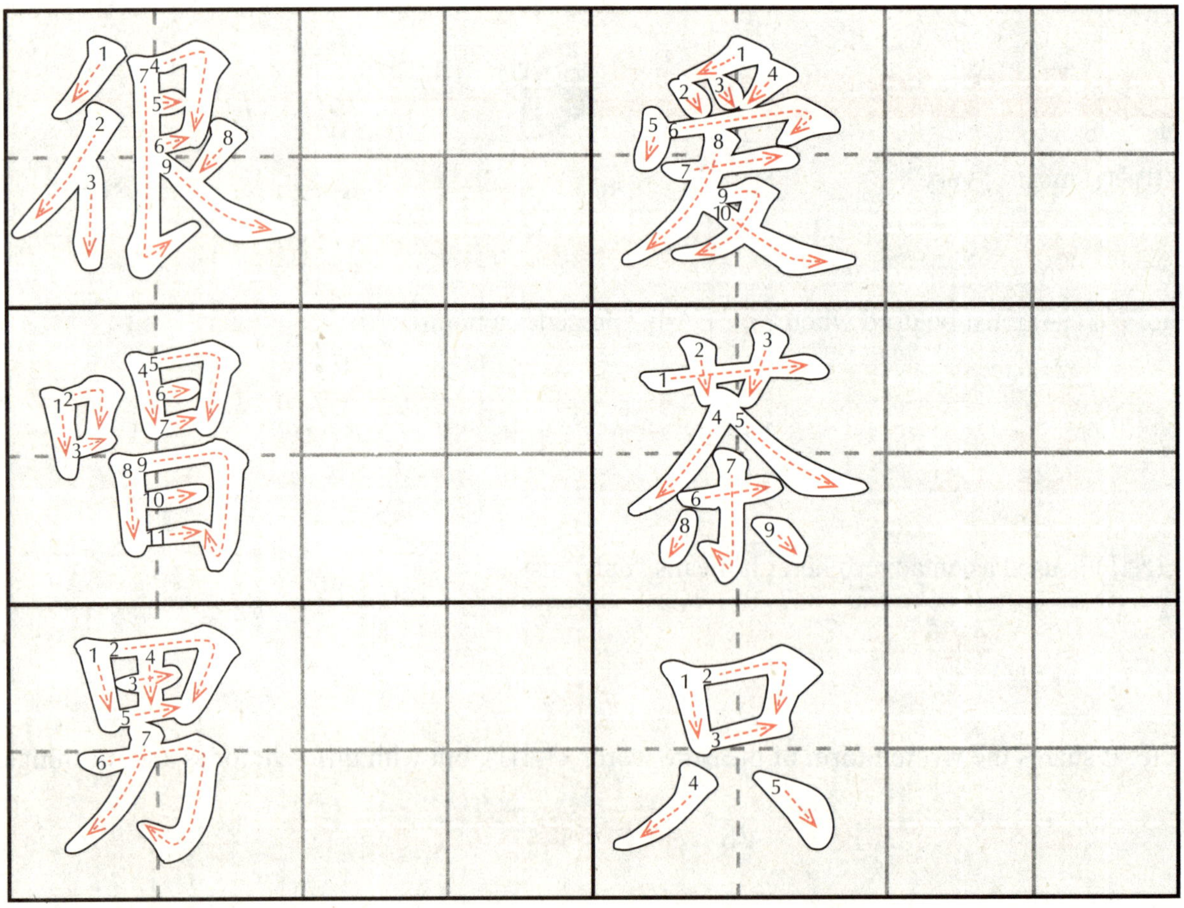

很 爱
唱 茶
男 只

Unit 4
The Family 家人

Ex. 4.25   Homework. Translate the following sentences into Chinese.

1. I love to drink Chinese tea.

2. My father drinks only very good English tea.

3. I love my home very much.

4. The male teacher loves his family very much.

5. America is very beautiful, and American women are also pretty.

Culture factor

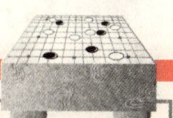

Tea originates from China. China has many different kinds of tea: jasmine tea (huāchá), green tea (lǜchá), chrysanthemum tea (júhuāchá), etc. The word "tea" in English actually comes from a word in a southern Chinese dialect that has a similar pronunciation. Also, as you may already know, another way to say tea is "cha", and the sound is taken from northern Chinese dialects.

Useful expressions

请进！	Qǐng jìn.	Come in, please.
请坐！	Qǐng zuò.	Sit down, please.
请喝茶！	Qǐng hē chá.	Please have some tea.

Unit 5
My Birthday 我的生日

In this unit you will learn:

- more numbers
- days of the week
- months and years
- how to express dates

Task 1   八月七号是我的生日

月	yuè	month, moon
号	hào	date, number
日	rì	day, date, sun
朋	péng	friend
友	yǒu	friend

Ex. 5.1   Listen to the recording carefully.

大家好！我姓王，叫王月美。八月七号是我的生日。

我有一个妹妹，她叫美英。她的生日是四月二十六号。

我妈妈的生日是五月十九日。爸爸的生日是二月二十八日。我有一个好朋友，她也姓王。她的生日是三月十二日。我的朋友，你的生日是几月几号？

Unit 5
My Birthday 我的生日

Ex. 5.2 Choose the right English meanings to fill in the blanks.

> friend   good friend   girl friend
> day, date, sun   which day   month, moon
> which month   birthday   the 24th of (month)
> give birth; person   date, number   which month and which day

1.	yuè	月	
2.	rì	日	
3.	hào	号	
4.	èrshísì rì/ hào	二十四日/号	
5.	shēng	生	
6.	shēngri	生日	
7.	péngyou	朋友	
8.	nǚ péngyou	女朋友	
9.	hǎo péngyou	好朋友	
10.	jǐ yuè	几月	
11.	jǐ hào	几号	
12.	jǐ yuè jǐ hào	几月几号	

Ex. 5.3 Listen to the wordlist and check your answers, then listen to the recording again and choose the right birthdays to fill in the blanks.

> 五月十九号/日   八月七号/日   四月二十六号/日
> 三月十二号/日   二月二十八号/日

Person	Birthday	
王月美	月	号/日
王美英	月	号/日
王月美的妈妈	月	号/日
王月美的爸爸	月	号/日
王月美的好朋友	月	号/日

Grammar Notes   Expressing time (1)

Chinese people express time by saying the month first and then the date. For expressing a month, you can simply put a number from 1-12 in front of 月(yuè), i.e. 二月, 十二月. For the date, you may notice that there are two different ways to indicate dates, 日(rì) is for the written form while 号(hào) is more colloquial. 日 and 号 can be left out if the date is a number over 10.

Ex. 5.4 How do you say the following dates in Chinese?

1st of January   14th of February   16th of August
4th of October   30th of November   22nd of December

Ex. 5.5 Challenge questions.

1. Can you tell the difference between 一个月 and 一月?
2. How to say February and December?
3. How to say two months and twelve months?
4. How to say "this month"?

Ex. 5.6 Listening exercise. Choose the correct dates according to the recording.

1. A. 十月十号   B. 四月十号   C. 十月四号
2. A. 一月七日   B. 七月一日   C. 七月十一日
3. A. 三月十七日   B. 七月十三日   C. 十月十三日
4. A. 九月六号   B. 六月十九号   C. 九月十九号
5. A. 五月五日   B. 五月十五日   C. 四月五日

Ex. 5.7 Pair work.

Exchange information about your friends' birthday dates. Fill in the following table with the information you receive. Use the following questions:

Unit 5
My Birthday 我的生日

Q: 你的朋友叫什么？
A: ……
Q: 他/她的生日是几月几号？
A: ……

Card A

	我的朋友	他/她的生日是	你的朋友	他/她的生日是
1.	小龙	九月十五号		
2.	大牛	二月十七号		
3.	水月	七月三十号		

Card B

	我的朋友	他/她的生日是	你的朋友	他/她的生日是
1.	英英	一月八号		
2.	家美	十月十六号		
3.	大山	四月七号		

Ex. 5.8 Character practice. Copy each character 4 times in the boxes provided.

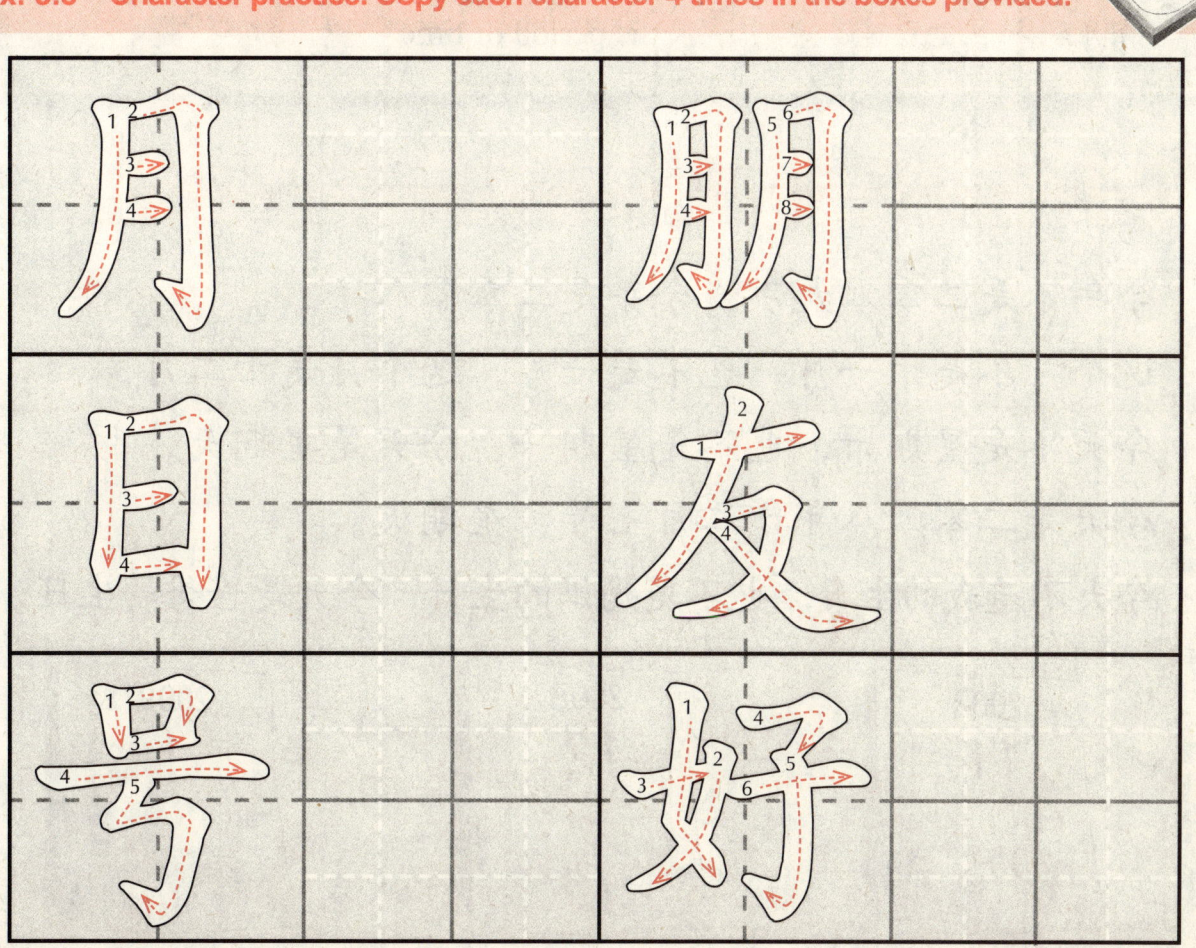

Ex. 5.9 Homework. Translate the following sentences into Chinese.

1. My elder sister's birthday is on the 31st of December.
   _____

2. My friend, when is your birthday?
   _____

3. She is my old friend, and she is also my very good friend.
   _____

Task 2   今天是星期天

今	jīng	the present time; now
年	nián	year
零	líng	zero
星	xīng	star
期	qī	the period of time

Ex. 5.10 Listen to the recording and circle today's date on the calendar.

今年不是二零零九年，今年是二零零八年。

这个月不是十一月，也不是一月，这个月是十二月。

今天不是星期六，也不是星期一，今天是星期天。

今天是二零零八年十二月七号，星期天。

今天不是我的生日，也不是妈妈的生日，今天是爸爸的生日。

Unit 5
My Birthday 我的生日

Ex. 5.11 Choose the right English meanings to fill in the blanks.

week	Monday	Sunday	this month
day	today	year	this year
2008	2009	January	December
zero	star	date	now, present

1.	jīn	今	
2.	tiān	天	
3.	jīntiān	今天	
4.	nián	年	
5.	jīnnián	今年	
6.	líng	零	
7.	èr líng líng bā	二零零八	
8.	èr líng líng jiǔ	二零零九	
9.	zhège yuè	这个月	
10.	yī yuè	一月	
11.	shí'èr yuè	十二月	
12.	xīng	星	
13.	qī	期	
14.	xīngqī	星期	
15.	Xīngqīyī	星期一	
16.	Xīngqītiān	星期天	

Ex. 5.12 Listen to the wordlist and check your answers.

Grammar Notes Expressing time (2)

1. Chinese list the date from the biggest concept to the smallest concept. i.e., year-month-day, and day of the week.

  ▶ Friday, 8th of August, 2008   二零零八年八月八日，星期五

2. To express a year, just read out the numbers one by one and then add 年 (nián). For example: 1789 年 is "yī qī bā jiǔ nián".

3. For showing the day of the week, simply put a number from 1 to 6 after the 星期 (xīngqī).

65

Please pay attention that Sunday is 星期天(Xīngqītiān) or 星期日(Xīngqīrì).

▶ 星期一　　星期二　　星期三　　星期四　　星期五　　星期六
　星期日/星期天

Ex. 5.13 Read out the following time expressions and state their meanings.

| 1776年 | 1949年 | 1911年 | 2000年 | 2008年 |
| 一月 | 四月 | 七月 | 九月 | 十月 |

Ex. 5.14 Do you know the meanings of the following expressions?

星期一	一个星期	一个星期一
一个月	一月	两个月
一天	一年	两个星期
水星	火星	日期

Ex. 5.15 Can you read out the following dates in Chinese as quickly and accurately as possible?

例：　Sunday, 7th of December, 2008 → 二零零八年十二月七号, 星期天

1. Friday, 12th of October, 2007
2. Saturday, 24th of November, 2007
3. Friday, 2nd of May, 2008
4. Thursday, 25th of December, 2008
5. Monday, 5th of January, 2009
6. Sunday, 21th of June, 2009

Ex. 5.16 Listening exercise. Listen to the recording and circle the correct answers.

1. A. 二零零六年　　　B. 二零六零年　　　C. 二六零零年

Unit 5
My Birthday 我的生日

2. A. 星期一 　　　　　 B. 星期二 　　　　　 C. 星期日
3. A. 十个月 　　　　　 B. 十月 　　　　　　 C. 十二月
4. A. 九月十八日 　　　 B. 八月十九日 　　　 C. 八月十八日
5. A. 一九九七年七月七号 　　　　　　　　 B. 一九七七年十月十号
6. A. 一九四九年十月一日 　　　　　　　　 B. 一九一一年十月十日

Ex. 5.17 Character practice. Copy each character 4 times in the boxes provided.

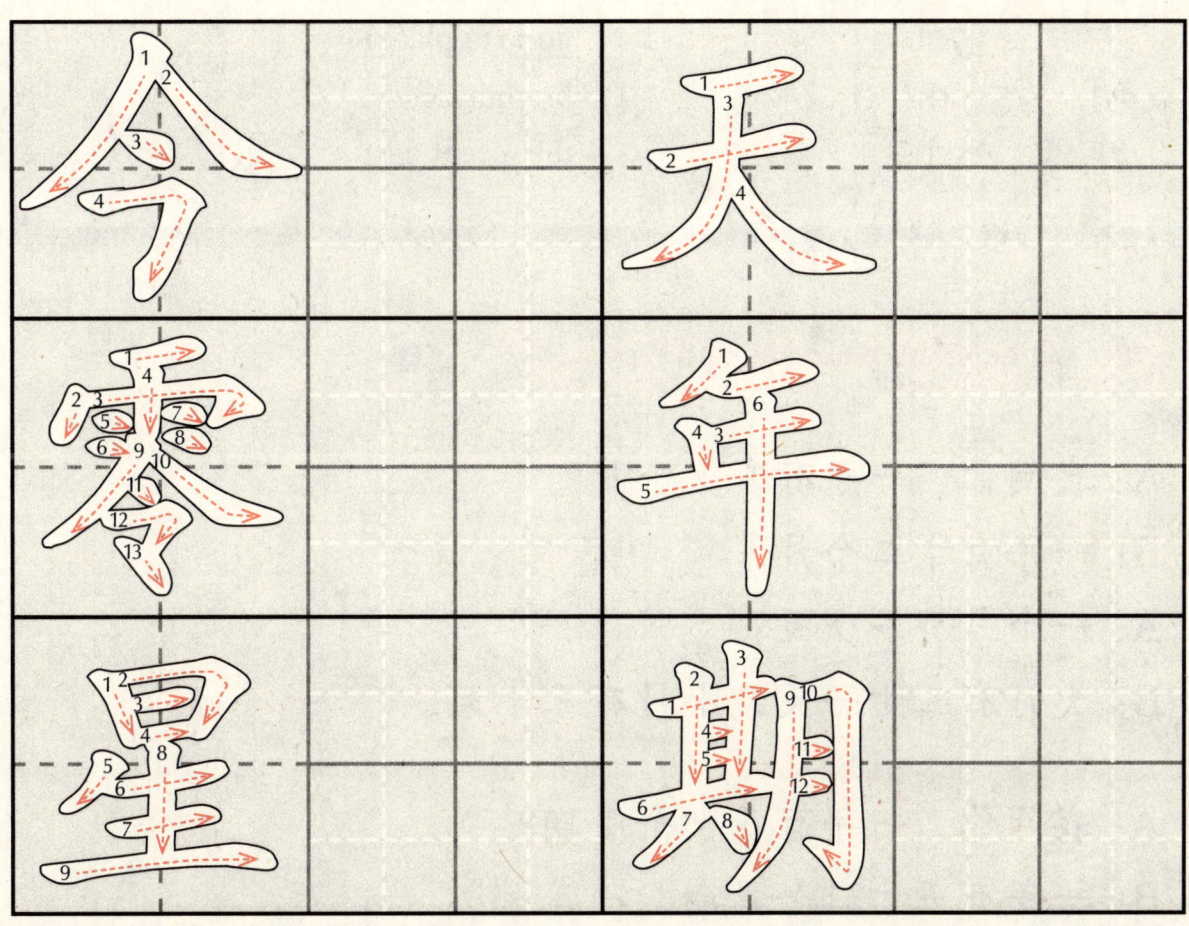

Ex. 5.18 Homework. Copy the following questions and answer them in Chinese.

1. 今年是二零零几年?
2. 今天是星期几?

3. 这个月是几月?
4. 今天是几月几号?
5. 你的生日是几月几号?

Task 3 我问你

问	wèn	ask
多	duō	many, much
少	shǎo	few
去	qù	go to (a place)
明	míng	brightness
昨	zuó	the recent past

Ex. 5.19 Listen to the recording and repeat.

A: 我问你,一年有多少个月?

B: 一年有十二个月。

A: 一个月有多少天?

B: 大月有三十一天,小月有三十天。

A: 我问你,一年有多少个星期?

B: 一年有五十二个星期。

A: 一个星期有几天?

B: 一个星期有七天。星期一、星期二、星期三、星期四、星期五、星期六、星期天。

A: 我问你,今年是二零零几年?

B: 今年是二零零八年。

Unit 5
My Birthday 我的生日

A：那去年呢？明年呢？

B：去年是二零零七年，明年是二零零九年。

A：我问你，今天是十一月二十八号星期五，昨天呢？明天呢？

B：昨天是十一月二十七号星期四。明天是十一月二十九号星期六。

Ex. 5.20 Choose the right English meanings to fill in the blanks.

ask	I ask you	that; so; in that case	today
big month	small month	yesterday	how many/much
tomorrow	this year	last year	next year
many, much	few	you ask me	go to

1.	wèn	问	
2.	wǒ wèn nǐ	我问你	
3.	nǐ wèn wǒ	你问我	
4.	nà	那	
5.	dà yuè	大月	
6.	xiǎo yuè	小月	
7.	jīntiān	今天	
8.	míng	明	brightness
9.	míngtiān	明天	
10.	zuó	昨	the recent past
11.	zuótiān	昨天	
12.	jīnnián	今年	
13.	míngnián	明年	
14.	qù	去	
15.	qùnián	去年	
16.	duō	多	
17.	shǎo	少	
18.	duōshao	多少	

Ex. 5.21 Listen to the wordlist and check your answers.

Grammar Notes 多少 & 几

1. 多少 (duōshao) and 几 (jǐ) are both used to ask "how many" and "how much". 多 means "lot, many" and 少 means "little, few". Together, 多少 is usually used for numbers over 10, while 几 is generally used for 10 and numbers less than 10.

   Q: 一个星期有几天？
   A: 一个星期有七天。
   Q: 一个月有多少天？
   A: 有的有二十天，有的有三十天，有的有三十一天。

2. For a number more than X, but less than Y, the expression is X 多 or X 几.

   more than 10, but less than 20   十多，十几
   more than 20, but less than 30   二十多，二十几
   more than 80, but less than 90   八十多，八十几

Ex. 5.22 Choose 多少 or 几 to ask questions. Write down the questions that you make.

1. 一年有十二个月。
2. 他家有六口人。
3. 哥哥有一只狗。
4. 中国有很多人。
5. 我有二十五个老师。

Ex. 5.23 Read out the following questions and answer them in Chinese as quickly as possible.

1. 今天是星期几？
2. 明天是星期几？昨天呢？
3. 这个月是几月？这个月有多少天？
4. 今年是二零零几年？
5. 今天是几月几号？
6. 你的生日是几月几号？

Unit 5
My Birthday 我的生日

7. 一年有多少个星期?
8. 一个星期有几天?
9. 这个星期五是几月几号?
10. 二零零八年八月八号是星期几?

Ex. 5.24 Character practice. Copy each character 4 times in the boxes provided.

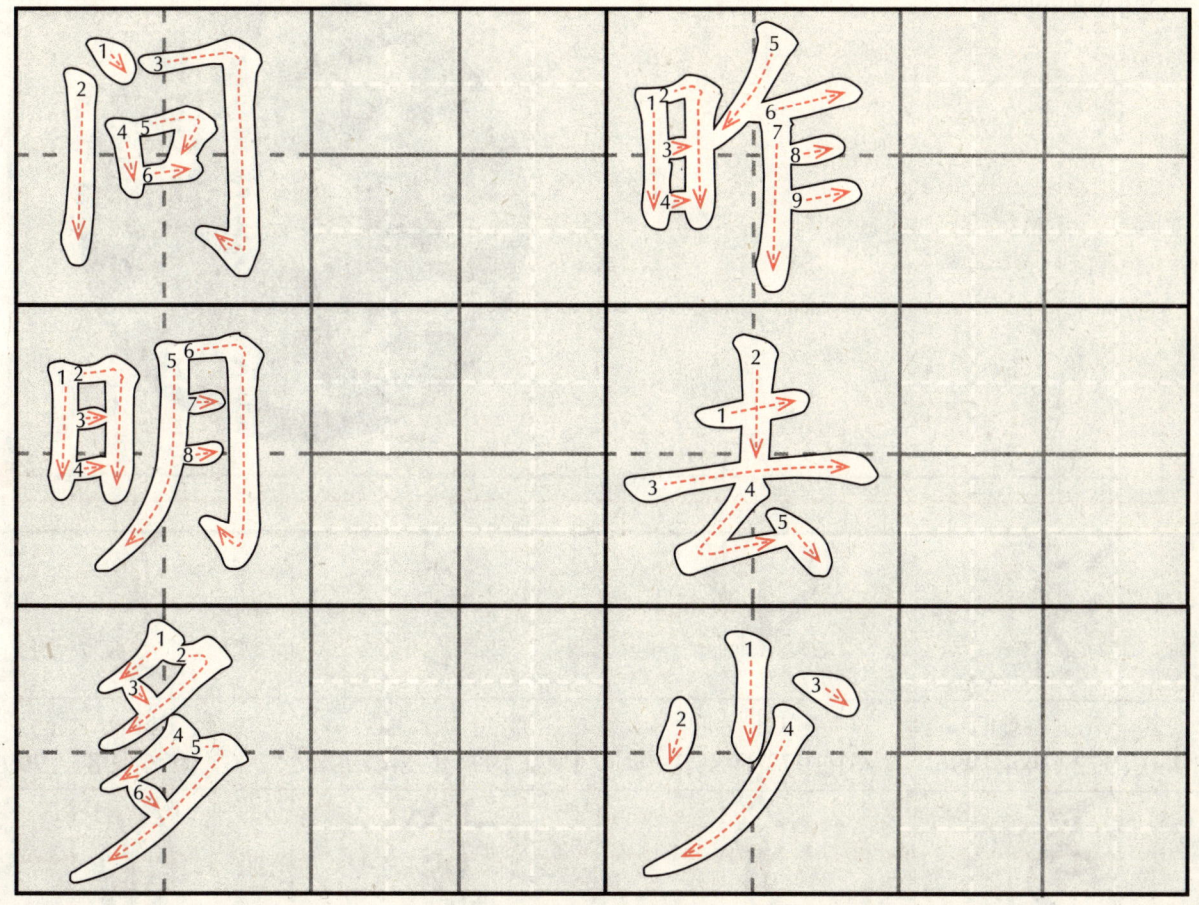

Ex. 5.25 Homework. Make up sentences by using the words/phrases provided, and then translate them into English.

1. 王　　　喝　　　　茶　　　爱　　　老师
2. 是　　　今天　　　生日　　你　　　的　　　吗
3. 多少　　一年　　　星期　　有　　　个
4. 生日　　这个　　　谁的　　星期六　是
5. 今天　　二十八号　是　　　星期五　十一月

Culture factor

The Chinese Zodiac has 12 animals. They are the Mouse, Ox, Tiger, Rabbit, Dragon, Snake, Horse, Ram, Monkey, Rooster, Dog and Pig. They represent a 12-year cycle. The first day of the Chinese lunar calendar generally falls somewhere between late January and early February. Since 1911 China has been using the Western calendar, but the lunar calendar is still used for festive occasions such as the Spring Festival. Have a look and see what your and your family's Chinese Zodiac animals are.

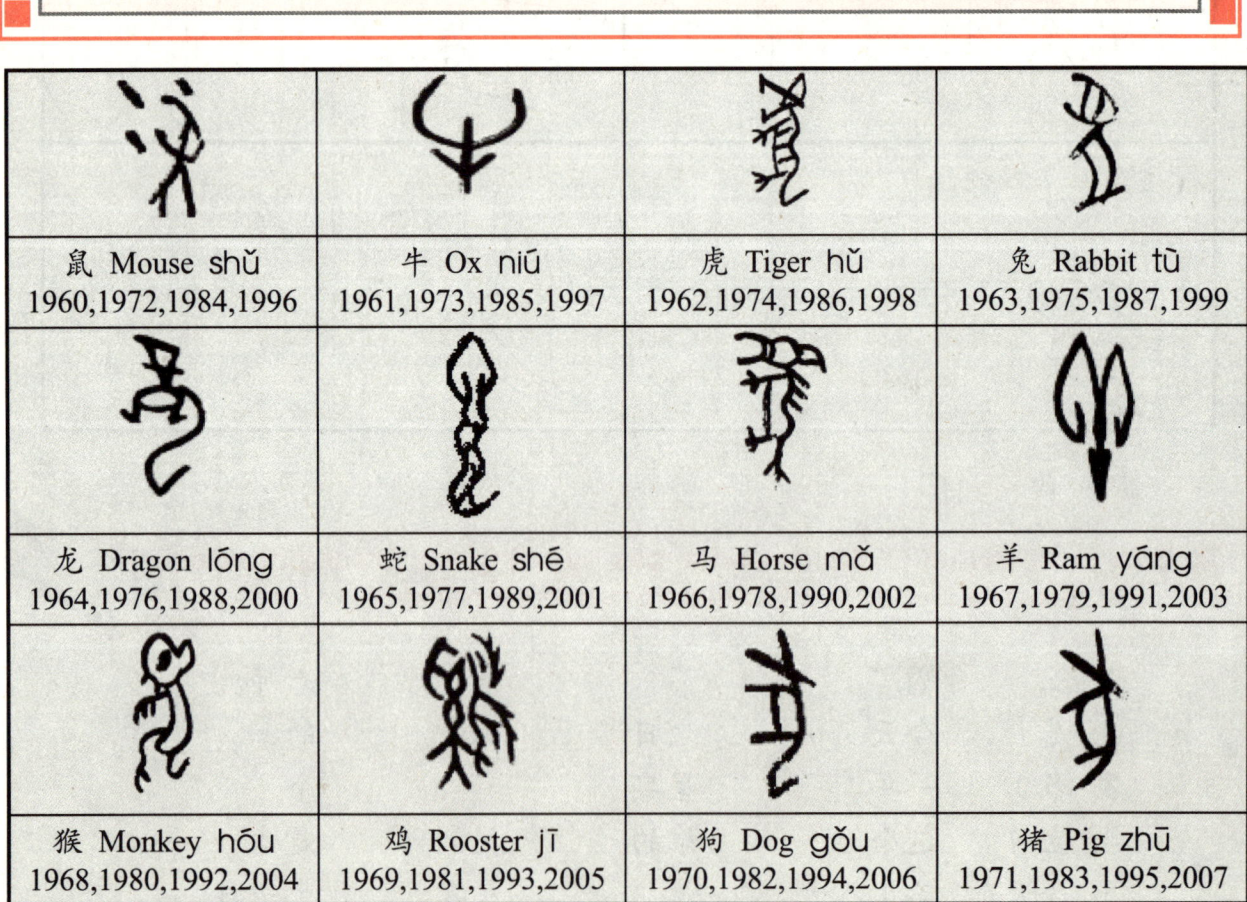

鼠 Mouse shǔ 1960,1972,1984,1996	牛 Ox niú 1961,1973,1985,1997	虎 Tiger hǔ 1962,1974,1986,1998	兔 Rabbit tù 1963,1975,1987,1999
龙 Dragon lóng 1964,1976,1988,2000	蛇 Snake shé 1965,1977,1989,2001	马 Horse mǎ 1966,1978,1990,2002	羊 Ram yáng 1967,1979,1991,2003
猴 Monkey hóu 1968,1980,1992,2004	鸡 Rooster jī 1969,1981,1993,2005	狗 Dog gǒu 1970,1982,1994,2006	猪 Pig zhū 1971,1983,1995,2007

Unit 5
My Birthday 我的生日

Useful expressions

你多大？	Nǐ duō dà ?	How old are you?
你今年多大？	Nǐ jīnnián duō dà ?	How old are you this year?
你属什么？	Nǐ shǔ shénme?	What is your Chinese Zodiac animal?
我属 X。	Wǒ shǔ X.	My Chinese Zodiac animal is X.
祝你生日快乐！	Zhù nǐ shēngri kuàilè!	Happy birthday to you!

73

Revision Unit 1

Pinyin Review

Here are two poems that cover a wide range of Chinese initials and finals. Please read them out loudly.

早 梅 诗
Zǎo Méi Shī

东 风 破 早 梅，
Dōng fēng pò zǎo méi,
向 暖 一 枝 开。
xiāng nuǎn yì zhī kāi.
冰 雪 无 人 见，
Bīng xuě wú rén jiàn,
春 从 天 上 来。
chūn cóng tiānshang lái.

Early Plum Blossom

(Translated by Jonny Moses)

The East wind scatters the early blossom,

seeking warmth, a flower unfurls from its bud.

Ice and snow now nowhere to be seen,

as Spring falls upon us from above.

捕 鱼
Bǔ Yú

人 远 江 空 夜，
Rén yuǎn jiāng kōng yè,
浪 滑 一 舟 轻。
làng huá yì zhōu qīng.
儿 咏 诶 唷 调，
Ér yǒng ē yō diào,
橹 和 哎 啊 声。
lǔ hé āi a shēng.

Fishing

(Translated by Jonny Moses)

The dead of night, alone on the empty river;

a single boat glides over the dark glazed sheet.

Silent, save the sound of an infant's "ay oh"

as the boatman's oar paddles out the beat.

Revision Unit 1

网罩波心月，
Wǎng zhào bō xīn yuè,
竿穿水面云。
gān chuān shuǐ miàn yún.
鱼虾留瓮内，
Yú xiā liú wèng nèi,
快活四时春。
kuàihuo sì shí chūn.

Fisher's net traps the Moon while it glimmers through the waves;

with his rod, spears a cloud, as it darts on the surface.

The prawns and the fish now lay rest in his casket;

fisher's life is cheerful and joyous as pleasant Spring time.

Character Revision

1. Combine the character in the centre with one of the characters in the square to create a character that matches the meaning given. These are all characters you have already learnt.

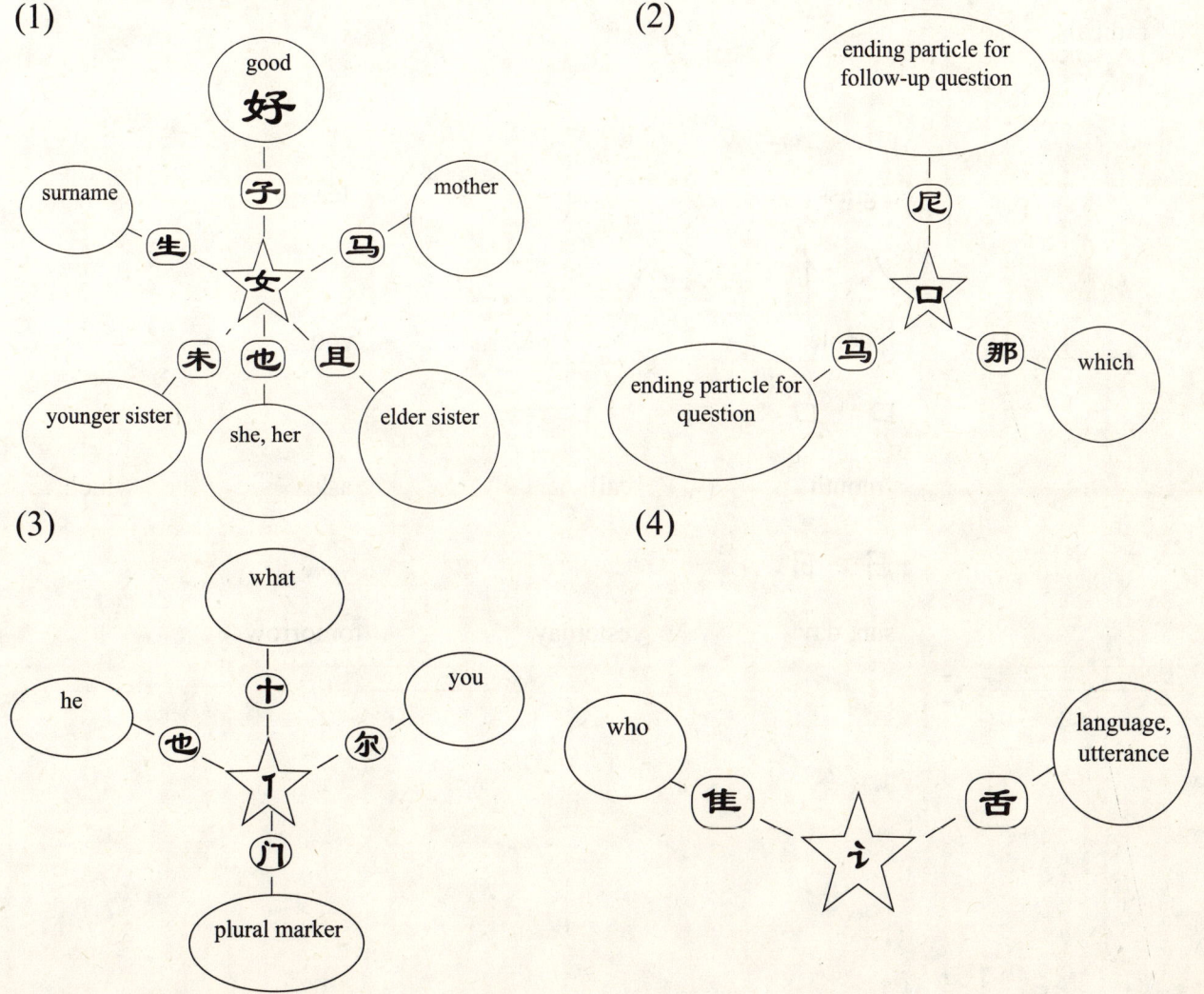

(1), (2), (3), (4)

2. Draw lines to link an upper part with a lower part of a character. This will create a character that you have already learnt. Write these three characters in the boxes.

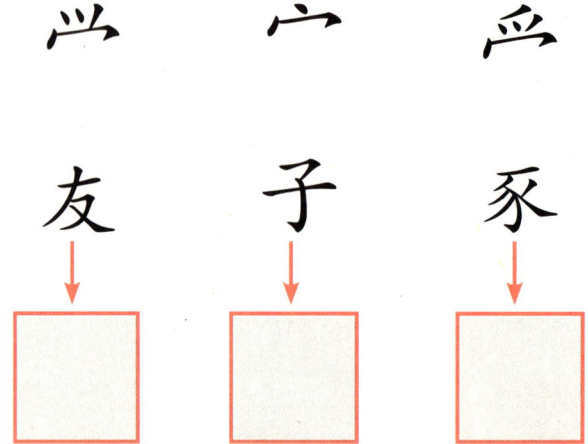

3. Write the Chinese characters according to the meaning provided. You will find that characters in each group share common components as shown on the left. These components are called radicals.

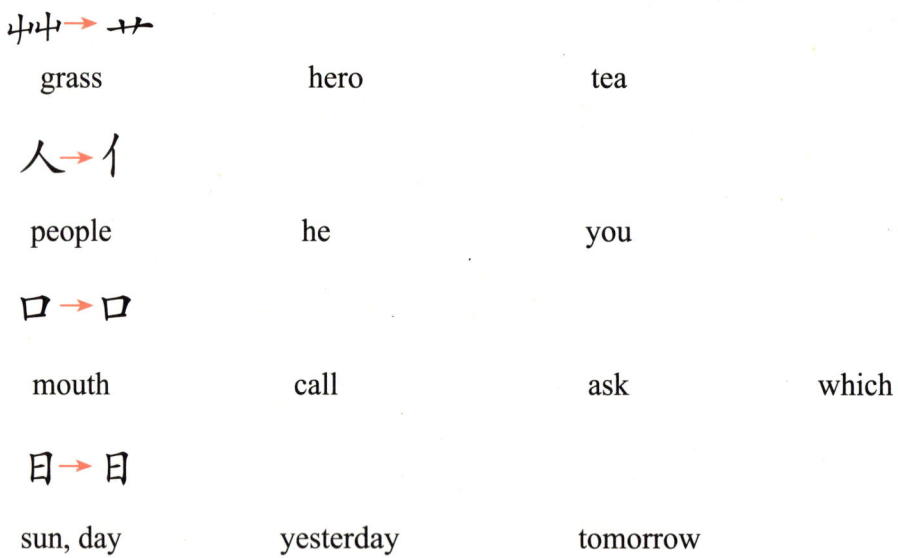

Progress Test 1 (Unit1T1- Unit4T1)

1. Translate the following words into English. (20%)

(1) 山 _____ 水 _____ 日 _____ 月 _____

(2) 龙 _____ 马 _____ 人 _____ 家 _____

(3) 美 _____ 好 _____ 大 _____ 小 _____

(4) 山羊 _____ 水牛 _____ 火山 _____ 国王 _____

(5) 两只狗 _____ 五只羊 _____ 九个弟弟 _____ 六口人 _____

(6) 中国 _____ 你好 _____ 女王 _____ 王国 _____

(7) 七十八 _____ 四十六 _____ 九十九 _____ 十二 _____

(8) 姓 _____ 是 _____ 叫 _____ 有 _____

(9) 哥哥 _____ 妹妹 _____ 姐姐 _____ 弟弟 _____

(10) 这 _____ 那 _____ 什么 _____ 哪 _____

2. Translate the following sentences into English. (30%)

(1) 他是英国人。 _____

(2) 这是美国。 _____

(3) 我是中国人。　＿＿＿＿＿＿＿＿＿＿＿＿＿＿＿
(4) 那不是我的电话。　＿＿＿＿＿＿＿＿＿＿＿＿＿＿＿
(5) 这是英国电话吗？　＿＿＿＿＿＿＿＿＿＿＿＿＿＿＿
(6) 谁有两个弟弟？　＿＿＿＿＿＿＿＿＿＿＿＿＿＿＿
(7) 你有没有狗？　＿＿＿＿＿＿＿＿＿＿＿＿＿＿＿
(8) 小水的爸爸有一个好电话。　＿＿＿＿＿＿＿＿＿＿＿＿＿＿＿
(9) 这是什么？　＿＿＿＿＿＿＿＿＿＿＿＿＿＿＿
(10) 这两个人是好人。　＿＿＿＿＿＿＿＿＿＿＿＿＿＿＿
(11) 你有几个妹妹？　＿＿＿＿＿＿＿＿＿＿＿＿＿＿＿
(12) 她姓王吗？　＿＿＿＿＿＿＿＿＿＿＿＿＿＿＿
(13) 谁的电话好？　＿＿＿＿＿＿＿＿＿＿＿＿＿＿＿
(14) 妈妈有电话吗？　＿＿＿＿＿＿＿＿＿＿＿＿＿＿＿
(15) 你家有几口人？　＿＿＿＿＿＿＿＿＿＿＿＿＿＿＿
(16) 我妈妈没有姐姐，她有一个哥哥。　＿＿＿＿＿＿＿＿＿＿＿＿＿＿＿
(17) 我的妹妹叫小水。　＿＿＿＿＿＿＿＿＿＿＿＿＿＿＿
(18) 谁是他爸爸？　＿＿＿＿＿＿＿＿＿＿＿＿＿＿＿
(19) 英国女王叫什么？　＿＿＿＿＿＿＿＿＿＿＿＿＿＿＿
(20) 这是你姐姐吗？　＿＿＿＿＿＿＿＿＿＿＿＿＿＿＿

3. Translate the following passages into English. (20%)

(1) 你们好！我姓王，叫小英。我家有三口人：爸爸，妈妈，我。我爸爸是英国人，妈妈不是英国人，她是中国人。

＿＿＿＿＿＿＿＿＿＿＿＿＿＿＿＿＿＿＿＿＿＿＿＿＿＿＿＿＿＿＿＿＿＿＿＿

＿＿＿＿＿＿＿＿＿＿＿＿＿＿＿＿＿＿＿＿＿＿＿＿＿＿＿＿＿＿＿＿＿＿＿＿

(2) 英国不大。英国没有国王，有一个女王。英国女王有狗。她有两只英国大狗，她没有中国狗，没有美国狗。

＿＿＿＿＿＿＿＿＿＿＿＿＿＿＿＿＿＿＿＿＿＿＿＿＿＿＿＿＿＿＿＿＿＿＿＿

＿＿＿＿＿＿＿＿＿＿＿＿＿＿＿＿＿＿＿＿＿＿＿＿＿＿＿＿＿＿＿＿＿＿＿＿

4. Translate the following sentences into Chinese characters. (15%)

(1) I am American. _____

(2) This is my home. _____

(3) I don't have younger sister. _____

(4) Who doesn't have dog? _____

(5) That is my mother. _____

(6) Whose telephone is this? _____

(7) My father has two younger brothers. _____

(8) He doesn't have elder sister. _____

(9) I am called Little Water (Xiaoshui). _____

(10) Is he Chinese? _____

5. Answer the following questions with Chinese characters. (15%)

(1) Q: 你好！我叫大牛，你叫什么？
    A: _____

(2) Q: 我是中国人。你是哪国人？
    A: _____
    (use English names for your country if you are not British or American)

(3) Q: 我家有四口人。你家有几口人？
    A: _____

(4) Q: 我有一个妹妹，你有妹妹吗？
    A: _____

(5) Q: 我家没有狗，你家有没有狗？
    A: _____

Progress Test 2 (Unit1T1- Unit5T3)

1. Translate the following words into English. (20%)

(1) 日 _____ 月 _____ 火 _____ 山 _____

(2) 她 _____ 好 _____ 姓 _____ 妈 _____

(3) 男 _____ 中 _____ 多 _____ 少 _____

(4) 生日 _____ 好朋友 _____ 零零七 _____ 多大 _____

(5) 六口人 _____ 一个朋友 _____ 四个英国人 _____ 两只狗 _____

(6) 美国 _____ 星期六 _____ 中国茶 _____ 学生 _____

(7) 八月五号 _____ 七月六日 _____ 二月十八 _____ 三月三号 _____

(8) 爱 _____ 不学 _____ 问 _____ 喝 _____

(9) 今天 _____ 明天 _____ 去年 _____ 昨天 _____

(10) 那 _____ 这 _____ 谁 _____ 什么 _____

2. Translate the following into English (30%)

(1) 谁是中国老师？ _____

(2) 这是哪儿？ _____

(3) 今天是七月十八号。 _____

(4) 她也不是美国学生。 _____

(5) 这是谁的电话? _____

(6) 谁是你弟弟? _____

(7) 你爱喝茶吗? _____

(8) 小水的老师有一个儿子,他是中学生。 _____

(9) 明天是不是你的生日? _____

(10) 这茶很好,是中国茶吗? _____

(11) 你家谁爱喝英国茶? _____

(12) 昨天星期四,今天星期五。 _____

(13) 你今年多大? _____

(14) 一个月有多少天? _____

(15) 今天是二零零八年。 _____

3. Translate the following passages into English. (20%)

(1) 今天英国没有国王,只有一个女王。英国女王姓Windsor,叫Elisabeth。英国女王没有哥哥,也没有弟弟。女王只有一个妹妹,她叫Margaret。英国女王很爱狗。她有一只英国小狗,这是英国女王的狗,不是她妹妹的狗。英国女王爱喝茶,她不喝中国茶,只喝英国茶。

_____

_____

(2) 这两个人是我的中学老师。男老师是英国人,女老师也是英国人。他们都爱喝茶。今天星期一,男老师没有茶,他问女老师:"你有茶吗?"今天女老师也没有茶。这个星期一他们两个人没喝茶。

_____

_____

4. Translate the following into Chinese characters. (15%)

(1) That is my home. _____

(2) I don't have Chinese friend. _____

(3) Today is my birthday. _____

(4) This year is year 2008. _____

(5) Does this male teacher like tea? _____

(6) Whose telephone is this? _____

(7) When is his birthday? _____

(8) My father has two dogs. _____

(9) The male teacher loves his family very much. _____

(10) Are you English? _____

5. Answer the following questions with Chinese characters. (15%)

(1) Q: 你好！我是中国人。你是哪国人？
    A: _____

(2) Q: 你的生日是几月几号？
    A: _____

(3) Q: 我爱喝茶，你爱喝茶吗？
    A: _____

(4) Q: 今天星期一，明天呢？
    A: _____

(5) Q: 我问你，一个月有多少天？
    A: _____

Unit 6

Directions and Time
方向和时间

In this unit you will learn:

- points of the compass
- how to ask and tell the time
- how to say time periods: morning, noon and evening

Task 1　他们是中国人吗？

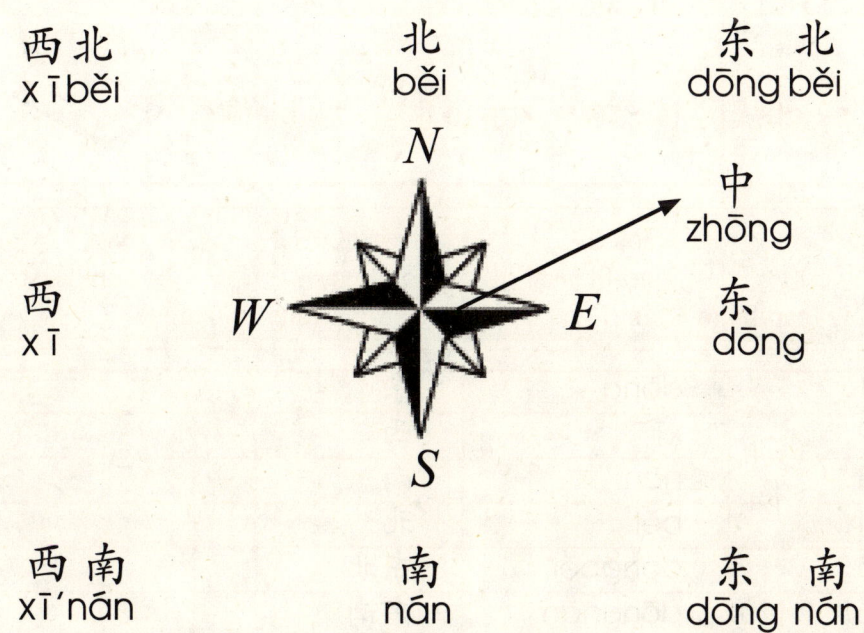

Ex. 6.1 Read the map and listen to the recording.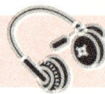

这是中国。中国很大，中国人也很多。

这三个人是中国人。一个是东北人，一个是西北人，一个是西南人。中国是她们的家。

这(A)是北京。北京很大，人很多。

这(B)是南京。南京不大，人也不多。

Ex. 6.2 Choose the right English meanings to fill in the blanks.

north	south	west	east
northwest	northeast	southwest	southeast
Beijing (capital of China)		Nanjing (city in China)	

1.	dōng	东	
2.	xī	西	
3.	nán	南	
4.	běi	北	
5.	dōngběi	东北	
6.	dōngnán	东南	
7.	xīběi	西北	
8.	xīnán	西南	
9.	jīng	京	capital (city)
10.	Běijīng	北京	
11.	Nánjīng	南京	

Unit 6
Directions and Time 方向和时间

Ex. 6.3 Listen to the wordlist and check your answers.

Ex. 6.4 Here is a map of China and Japan. Some characters in the cities' names are missing. Choose the right direction words to fill in the blanks.

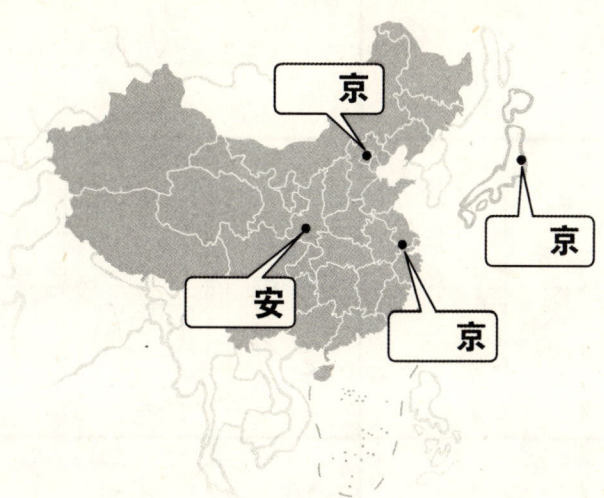

Ex. 6.5 Read out the following directions.

1. 这是  。

2. 这是  。

3. 这是  。

4. 这是  。

5. 这是  。

6. 这是  。

7. 这是  。

8. 这是  。

Ex. 6.6 Character practice. Copy each character 4 times in the boxes provided.

Ex. 6.7 Homework.

1. Translate the following phrases and sentences into English.

   西北_____　中东_____　北美_____　南美_____

   这是北京，北京很大，有很多人。
   _____

   那是东京，东京的中国人不多。
   _____

2. Translate the following sentences into Chinese.

   (1) Where are you from?　_____

   (2) I am from China.　_____

Unit 6
Directions and Time 方向和时间

(3) I am from Beijing, China. (=I am Chinese.) _____

(4) His father is from the UK. _____

(5) Her mother is from the United States. _____

Task 2 现在几点？

现	xiàn	at present
在	zài	be in/at/on
点	diǎn	o'clock
半	bàn	half
分	fēn	minute, cent

Ex. 6.8 Listen to the recording and repeat.

 现在几点？ 现在六点。

 现在几点？ 现在两点。

 现在几点？ 现在十一点。

 现在几点？ 现在十一点半。

 现在几点？ 现在六点十五（分）。

 现在几点？ 现在一点四十五（分）。

 现在几点？ 现在三点四十（分）。

Ex.6.9 Choose the right English meanings to fill in the blanks.

	now	o'clock, point	which o'clock; what time
	eleven o'clock	forty-five minutes	what time is it now
	minute	half	eleven thirty
	two o'clock		

1.	zài	在	be in/ at/ on
2.	xiàn	现	at present
3.	xiànzài	现在	
4.	diǎn	点	
5.	jǐ diǎn	几点	
6.	xiànzài jǐ diǎn	现在几点	
7.	shíyī diǎn	十一点	
8.	liǎng diǎn	两点	
9.	bàn	半	
10.	shíyī diǎn bàn	十一点半	
11.	fēn	分	
12.	sìshíwǔ fēn	四十五分	

Ex. 6.10 Listen to the wordlist and check your answers.

Grammar Notes   Sentences indicating time

1. You may notice that in sentences indicating time, sometimes the verb 是 is optional.

现在几点?　　现在两点半。
现在是七点五十五，不是八点。

Ex. 6.11 Can you read out the following sentences? Please notice the verb 是 is optional.

1. 今天(是) 几号?　　　　　　　　　今天(是)十五号。
2. 今天(是)几月几号?　　　　　　　今天(是)四月十五号。

Unit 6
Directions and Time 方向和时间

3. 昨天(是) 星期几?   昨天(是)星期一。
4. 去年(是)二零零几年?   去年(是)二零零七年。
5. 现在(是) 几点?   现在(是)十二点半。
6. 这个月(是)几月? 下个月(是) 几月?   这个月(是)三月,下个月(是)四月。

Grammar Notes   Quarters and halves

1. If there are more than 10 minutes, 分 (fēn) can be dropped.

   八点五分   八点十分   八点十五(分)   八点五十五(分)

2. 30 minutes can be expressed as 半 (bàn) or 三十分 (sānshí fēn).

   两点半   两点三十(分)

3. 15 minutes can be expressed as 刻 (kè), this sound is borrowed from the English word "quarter" or 15 minutes.

   五点十五(分)/五点一刻   五点四十五(分)/五点三刻

Ex. 6.12   Can you read out the following times?

1.

2.

3.

Ex. 6.13 Can you write down the time shown on each clock in Chinese?

 1. _____  2. _____

 3. _____  4. _____

Ex. 6.14 Character practice. Copy each character 4 times in the boxes provided.

Unit 6
Directions and Time 方向和时间

Ex. 6.15 Homework. Translate the following sentences into Chinese.

1. What time is it now? _____

2. It is half past twelve. _____

3. It is ten to three. _____

Task 3　英国现在是晚上九点半

晚	wǎn	late
上	shàng	up, top
早	zǎo	early
下	xià	under, below
午	wǔ	noon

Ex. 6.16 Listen to the following dialogue carefully.

A: 英国现在几点？

B: 英国现在是星期六晚上九点半。

A: 北京现在几点？

B: 北京现在是星期天早上五点半。

A: 美国New York现在几点？

B: New York现在是星期六下午四点半。

Ex. 6.17 Choose the right English meanings to fill in the blanks.

early	late	noon	up, top
under, below	morning (before 8a.m.)		a.m. (8a.m.-12p.m.)
midday (12-2p.m.)	p.m. (2-6p.m.)		evening (6p.m.-)

1.	zǎo	早	
2.	shàng	上	
3.	zǎoshang	早上	
4.	wǎn	晚	
5.	wǎnshang	晚上	
6.	xià	下	
7.	wǔ	午	
8.	shàngwǔ	上午	
9.	zhōngwǔ	中午	
10.	xiàwǔ	下午	

Ex. 6.18 Listen to the wordlist and check your answers.

Ex. 6.19 Put the following times into the right time period columns.

| 1:20 p.m. | 12:00 p.m. | 9:15 a.m. | 2:00 p.m. |
| 7:30 a.m. | 10:00 p.m. | 7:45 p.m. | 6:00 p.m. |

早上	上午	中午	下午	晚上
		12:00 p.m.		

92

Unit 6
Directions and Time 方向和时间

Ex. 6.20 Choose card A or card B. Exchange information with your partner using the following pattern. Complete the time column with the information your partner provides.

Q: 北京现在几点?
A: 北京现在是星期天早上三点半。

例: Beijing 北京 Sun 3:30 a.m.

Card A

1.	Hong Kong	香港 Xiānggǎng	Sat 3:30 p.m.
2.	New York	纽约 Niǔyuē	
3.	Athens	雅典 Yǎdiǎn	Sat 10:30 p.m.
4.	London	伦敦 Lúndūn	
5.	Auckland	奥克兰 Àokèlán	Sun 7:30 p.m.
6.	Vancouver	温哥华 Wēngēhuá	

Card B

1.	Hong Kong	香港 Xiānggǎng	
2.	New York	纽约 Niǔyuē	Sat 2:30 p.m.
3.	Athens	雅典 Yǎdiǎn	
4.	London	伦敦 Lúndūn	Sat 8:30 p.m.
5.	Auckland	奥克兰 Àokèlán	
6.	Vancouver	温哥华 Wēngēhuá	Sat 11:30 a.m.

Ex. 6.21 Character practice. Copy each character 4 times in the boxes provided.

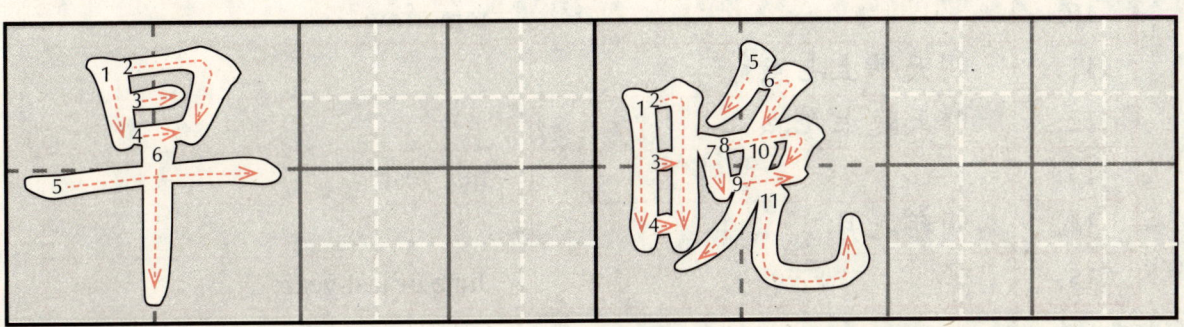

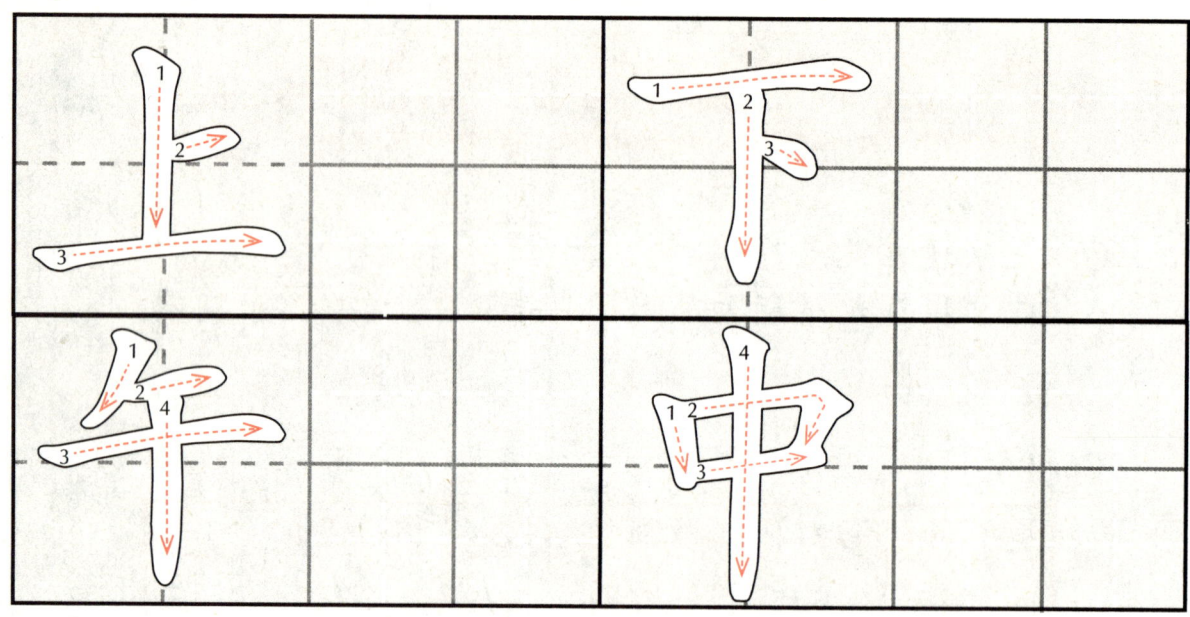

Ex. 6.22 Homework. Translate the following time expressions into Chinese or English.

	Chinese	English
1.		last week
2.	这个星期	
3.		next Friday
4.	上个星期四	
5.		this month
6.	上个月三号	
7.	下个月九号	
8.		today
9.	昨天	
10.		tomorrow
11.	明天早上七点	
12.	昨天晚上九点	
13.		this year
14.	明年七月	
15.		June of last year

Unit 6
Directions and Time 方向和时间

Culture factor

These are the official mascots of the Beijing 2008 Olympic Games, which will be held on 8th-24th August 2008. The design of these mascots is supposed to represent five little children who embody the Olympic Flame and four of China's most popular animals – the Fish, the Panda, the Tibetan Antelope and the Swallow.

Here are their names: the Fish is Beibei, the Panda is Jingjing, the Olympic Flame is Huanhuan, the Tibetan Antelope is Yingying, and the Swallow is Nini. When you put their names together – they are saying 北京欢迎你 (Běi Jīng Huān Yíng Nǐ), which means "Beijing Welcomes You" (Welcome to Beijing).

The image to the right is the logo for Beijing 2008. It shows a dancing character of 京.

Useful expressions

太好了!	Tài hǎo le!	Great!
真棒!	Zhēn bàng!	Fantastic!
请问，厕所在哪儿?	Qǐngwèn, cèsuǒ zài nǎr?	Excuse me, where is the lavatory?
对不起，我不知道。	Duìbuqǐ, wǒ bù zhīdào.	I am sorry, I don't know.

Unit 7

School (I) 学校（一）

In this unit you will learn:
- food and drink
- how to describe hobbies
- school life: teachers and lessons, subjects and timetable

Task 1 我们都喜欢吃中国饭

和	hé	and
都	dōu	all
喜	xǐ	be fond of; happiness
欢	huān	love, joy
吃	chī	eat
饭	fàn	cooked rice; meal, cuisine

Ex. 7.1 Listen to the recording carefully.

你们好！我叫明美。我家有五口人，爸爸、妈妈、哥哥、姐姐和我。我爸爸是中国人，妈妈是英国人。我是半个中国人，半个英国人。

我家人人都爱喝茶。我爸爸喜欢喝中国茶，他天天晚上都喝中国茶。妈妈爱喝英国茶，她天天早上都喝英国茶。

Unit 7
School (I) 学校（一）

我喜欢喝中国茶，也喜欢吃中国饭。我哥哥和姐姐也都喜欢吃中国饭。我们家星期六晚上吃中国饭。

Ex. 7.2 Choose the right English meanings to fill in the blanks.

> everyone / everyday / half (of) / all
> be fond of; happiness / love, like / and / Saturday
> cooked rice; meal, cuisine / eat / drink / drink tea

1.	bàn	半	
2.	rénrén	人人	
3.	tiāntiān	天天	
4.	xǐ	喜	
5.	huān	欢	love, joy
6.	xǐhuan	喜欢	
7.	hē	喝	
8.	hē chá	喝茶	
9.	chī	吃	
10.	fàn	饭	
11.	chī fàn	吃饭	eat a meal
12.	dōu	都	
13.	hé	和	
14.	Xīngqīliù	星期六	

Ex. 7.3 Listen to the wordlist and check your answers.

Ex. 7.4 Read the text and answer the following questions.

1. What's the girl's name?
2. What nationality is she?
3. How many family members does she have? Who are they?
4. What kind of tea does her father like to drink? When does he drink?

5. What kind of tea does her mother like to drink? When does she drink?
6. Who likes to eat Chinese food? When do they eat Chinese food?

Grammar Notes 都

1. 都(dōu) means "all", and it is used as an adverb in Chinese. It appears before verbs and often refers to the things in front of it.

   They are all Chinese.　　　　　　　他们都是中国人。
   I like both Chinese and English tea.　中国茶,英国茶我都喜欢。

2. Doubling up in the expression．天天(tiāntiān), 人人(rénrén), 家家(jiājiā) means "every", i.e. "every day", "everyone" and "every family" respectively. 都(dōu) is often used with this doubling up expression.

   Every family has a dog / dogs.　　家家都有狗。
   Everyone loves to drink tea.　　　人人都爱喝茶。
   They eat Chinese food every day.　他们天天都吃中国饭。

3. 都 (dōu) can be used with 也 (yě, also). Look at the following examples, pay attention to the usage of 也 and 也都．

   这个老师是英国人,那个学生也是英国人。
   老师都是英国人,学生也都是英国人。
   他很爱喝茶,我也很爱喝茶。
   他们很爱喝茶,我们也都很爱喝茶。

Ex. 7.5 Extra vocabulary – more beverages that you may 喝!

niúnǎi	牛奶	milk	jiǔ	酒	alcohol drinks
qìshuǐ	汽水	fizzy drinks	píjiǔ	啤酒	beer
shuǐ	水	water	hóngjiǔ	红酒	red wine
kělè	可乐	Coca-Cola	báijiǔ	白酒	white wine
guǒzhī	果汁	juice	kāfēi	咖啡	coffee

Unit 7
School (I) 学校(一)

Ex. 7.6 Pair work. Choose card A or card B. Ask your partner the following questions in turn. Write down the answers you get.

Card A

1. 你叫什么?_____
2. 你家有几口人?_____
3. 你喜欢吃什么?_____
4. 你爱吃中国饭吗?你为什么（不）爱吃中国饭?_____
5. 你喜欢喝什么?_____
6. 你天天都喝可乐(kělè)吗?_____
7. 你和你的家人都爱喝可乐吗?_____

Card B

1. 你有没有好朋友?_____
2. 你的好朋友叫什么?_____
3. 你的好朋友喜欢吃什么?_____
4. 你的好朋友爱吃中国饭吗?_____
5. 你的好朋友不喜欢喝什么?_____
6. 你的好朋友天天都喝茶吗?_____
7. 你和你的朋友都爱喝中国茶吗?_____

Ex. 7.7 Character practice. Copy each character 4 times in the boxes provided.

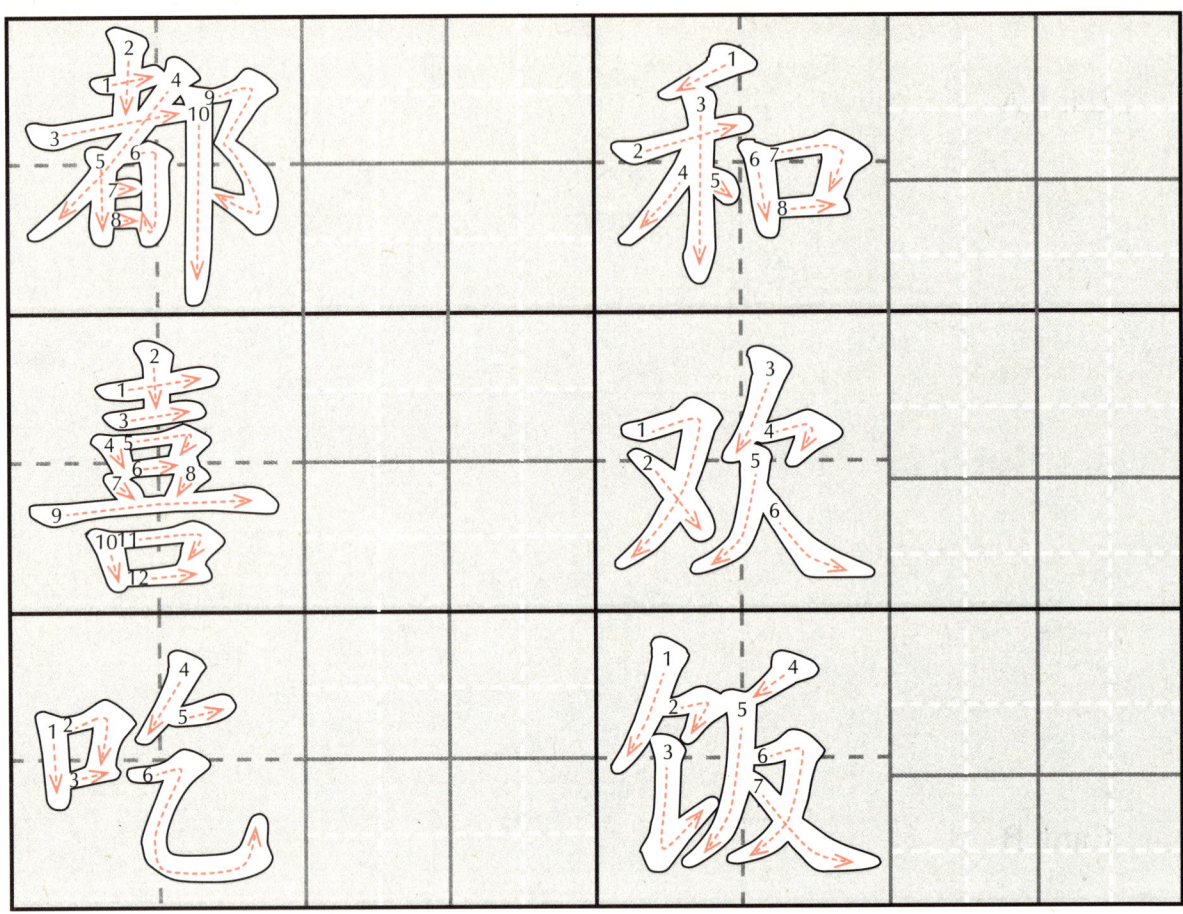

Ex. 7.8 Homework. Translate the following passage into Chinese.

1. There are 3 people in my family: father, mother and me.

2. My father is English, and he likes to drink English tea.

3. My mother is also English, but she doesn't like to drink tea.

4. She likes to eat food and loves to eat both Chinese food and English food.

5. I don't like tea. I only drink water.

Unit 7
School (I) 学校(一)

Task 2　我的中学

岁	suì	year of age
百	bǎi	hundred
外	wài	foreign, external
每	měi	every
课	kè	lesson, class

Ex. 7.9　Listen to the recording and repeat.

　　大家好！我是王学明，今年十四岁，现在是北星中学的学生。我的中学有八百多个学生；有男学生，也有女学生；有很多英国学生，也有二十几个外国学生。

　　我们中学有四十多个老师，男老师多，女老师少。我们的老师有的是英国人，有的是外国人。他们都是很好的老师。

　　我们每天早上八点半上课，下午四点半下课。每个星期上五天半课。星期六只上半天课。星期六下午和星期天都不上课。

Ex. 7.10 Choose the right English meanings to fill in the blanks.

every	hundred	year of age	year
student	teacher	foreign country	some
800	20+	half day	attend (class)
start/attend class	finish class	everyone	every week
foreign	class, lesson		

1.	dàjiā	大家	
2.	suì	岁	
3.	nián	年	
4.	xuésheng	学生	
5.	lǎoshī	老师	
6.	yǒude	有的	
7.	wài	外	
8.	wàiguó	外国	
9.	bǎi	百	
10.	bā bǎi	八百	
11.	èrshíjǐ	二十几	
12.	měi	每	
13.	měi gē xīngqī	每个星期	
14.	bàn tiān	半天	
15.	shàng	上	
16.	kè	课	
17.	shàng kè	上课	
18.	xià kè	下课	

Ex. 7.11 Listen to the wordlist and check your answers.

Grammar Notes Expressing number

1. 百 (bǎi) means "hundred". You can express big numbers as below:

> 100 一百
> 250 二/两百五(十)

307 三百零七
999 九百九十九

2. Combining two consecutive numbers is the way to express a rough number:

   five or six students   五六个学生
   seven or eight o'clock   七八点
   eight or nine countries   八九个国家

3. To express the numbers between X and Y, use the following way:

   20-30(student)   二三十(个学生)
   50-60(year of age)   五六十(岁)
   200-300(student)   二三百(个好老师)

4. 几 (jǐ) is used to ask how much/many for 10 and numbers less than 10. It also means "few, several" and can be used to express a rough number.

   less than 10 (teachers)   几(个老师)
   10-20 (teachers)   十几/多(个老师)
   several tens (dogs)   几十(只狗)
   several hundred (years)   几百(年)

Ex. 7.12 Use the tips in brackets to answer the following questions in Chinese.

1. 你有多少个好朋友？(more than 10, less than 20)

2. 你的中学有多少个学生？(more than 400, less than 500)

3. 你的中学有多少个女老师？(20 something)

4. 你每天几点上课？(between 9-10a.m.)

5. 你每天几点吃早饭？(between 7-8a.m.)

Ex. 7.13 Pair work. Choose card A or B, Ask questions in turns and answer them according to the text of Ex. 7.9.

Card A

1.	学明今年十几岁？
2.	学明的中学叫什么？
3.	这个中学的女老师多不多？
4.	学明的老师好不好？
5.	学生们星期天上课吗？

Card B

1.	学明姓什么？
2.	学明的中学有多少个学生？
3.	这个中学的学生都是英国人吗？
4.	这个中学的学生一个星期上几天课？
5.	学生们星期天上午上不上课？

Ex. 7.14 Character practice. Copy each character 4 times in the boxes provided.

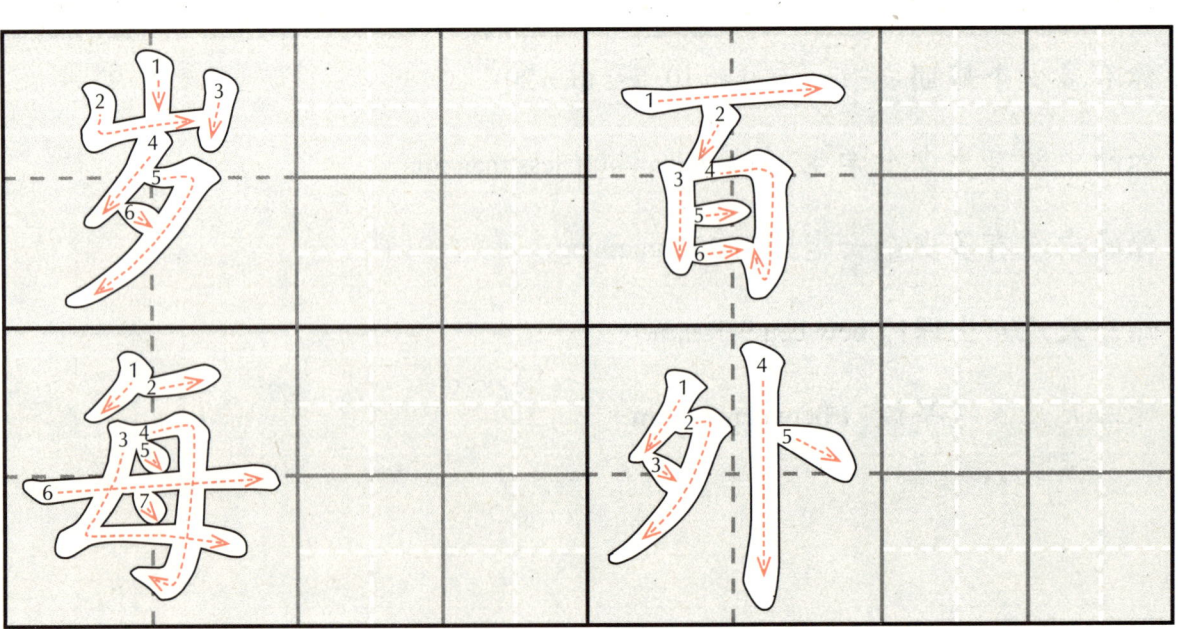

Unit 7
School (I) 学校(一)

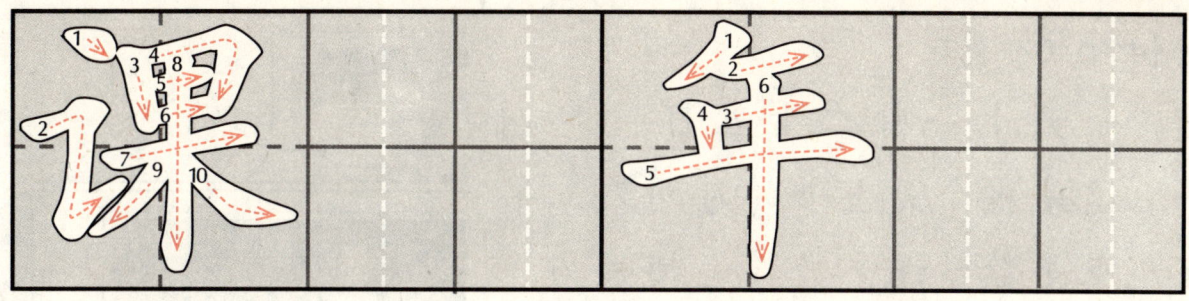

Ex. 7.15 Homework. Fill in the blanks according to the tips given in the brackets.

我姓_____(surname)，叫_____(first name)。我今年_____(age)岁。我是一个中学生。我的中学有_____(student's number)个学生。有男学生，_____(also)有女学生。有英国学生，也有_____(foreign)学生。我们中学也有很多老师，男老师_____(many)，女老师_____(few)。我们每个星期上_____(five)天课。星期六下午我们_____(don't)上课。星期天我们也不_____(attend class)。

Task 3   这是我的时间表

数	shū	number
化	huà	change, culture
文	wén	language; literary
时	shí	time
间	jiān	a unit (of time, space)
表	biǎo	chart, table, watch

Ex. 7.16 Listen to the recording carefully.

我的中学每个星期上五天课。我们每天早上九点上课。星期六和星期天我们不上课。我们学数学、化学，也学英文和外文。

今天十一月二十五日，星期一。这是我今天上午的时间表。早上九点是数学课。数学老师姓马。九点五十是英文课，英文老师是时老师。十一点是化学课。十一点五十我有文老师的中文课。

	十一月二十五号	星期一
9:00 - 9:40	数学	马老师
9:50-10:30	英文	时老师
11:00-11:40	化学	王老师
11:50-12:30	中文	文老师

Ex. 7.17 Choose the right English meanings to fill in the blanks.

time	have time (free)	do not have time	timetable
literature	mathematics	chemistry	English language
culture	foreign language	Teacher Shi	chart, table, watch
English literature	learn	Chinese language	Teacher Wen

1.	shí	时	time; also used as a surname
2.	wén	文	language; literary; a surname
3.	jiān	间	a unit (of time, space)
4.	shíjiān	时间	
5.	yǒu shíjiān	有时间	
6.	méiyǒu shíjiān	没有时间	
7.	biǎo	表	
8.	shíjiānbiǎo	时间表	
9.	xué	学	
10.	shù	数	number

Unit 7
School (I) 学校(一)

11.	shùxué	数学	
12.	huà	化	change, culture
13.	huàxué	化学	
14.	Yīngwén	英文	
15.	wàiwén	外文	
16.	Zhōngwén	中文	
17.	wénxué	文学	
18.	Yīngguó wénxué	英国文学	
19.	wénhuà	文化	
20.	Shí lǎoshī	时老师	
21.	Wén lǎoshī	文老师	

Ex. 7.18 Listen to the wordlist and check your answers.

Ex. 7.19 Read the text again, then read out the following questions and answer them in Chinese.

1. 今天是几月几号?
2. 这个学校星期六上课不上课?
3. 数学课几点上课? 数学老师是谁?
4. 英文课几点下课? 英文课的老师是谁?
5. 十一点是什么课? 老师是谁?
6. 今天有没有中文课? 中文老师是不是马老师?

Ex. 7.20 Extra vocabulary – more school subjects.

lìshǐ	历史	History	tǐyù	体育	P.E.
dìlǐ	地理	Geography	Fǎwén	法文	French
wùlǐ	物理	Physics	yìshù	艺术	Art
shēngwù	生物	Biology	yīnyuè	音乐	Music

Ex. 7.21 Pair work. Choose card A or B. Ask questions in turns and fill in the blanks with the information you get. Use the following patterns.

Q1: 你上午九点有什么课？

Q2: _____(subject)课的教师姓什么？

Card A

Time	Subject	Teacher
9:00—9:40		
9:45—10:20	数学	文老师
10:25—11:05		
10:05—12:45	化学	王老师
1:30—2:10		
2:15—2:55	中文	马老师

Card B

Time	Subject	Teacher
9:00—9:40	英文	时老师
9:45—10:20		
10:25—11:05	法文	牛老师
10:05—12:45		
1:30—2:10	英国文学	Smith老师
2:15—2:55		

Ex. 7.22 Character practice. Copy each character 4 times in the boxes provided.

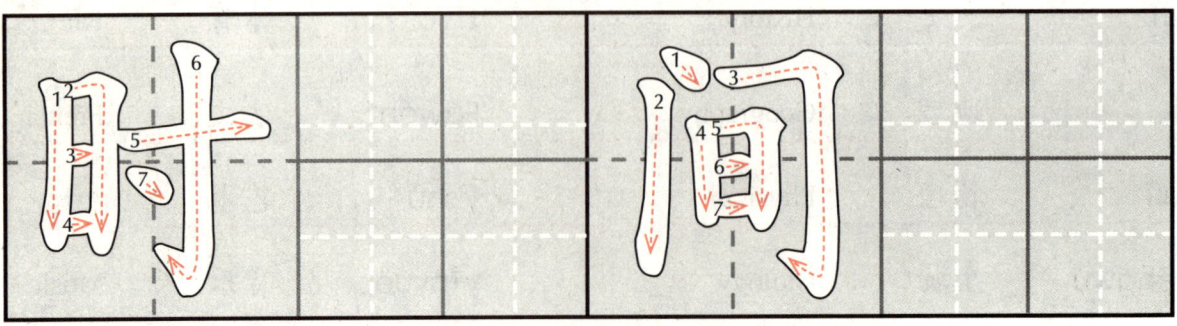

Unit 7
School (I) 学校(一)

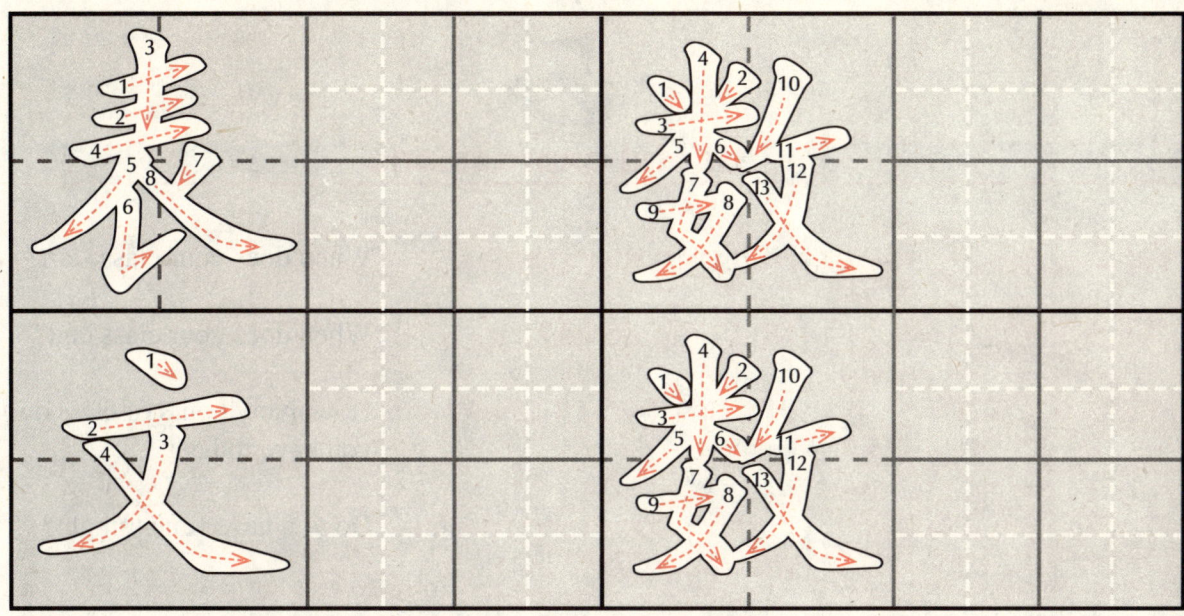

Ex. 7.23   Homework. Translate the following sentences into Chinese.

1. My little brother likes to learn mathematics and chemistry.   _____

2. My Chinese language teacher is called Teacher Shi.   _____

3. I have free time every Saturday afternoon.   _____

4. He has English literature class at 10:30.   _____

Culture factor

China is famous for four main ancient inventions. One is the compass, invented during China's Warring States Period (400 – 200 B.C.). Another is gunpowder, which changed war tactics around the world. Today, firecrackers are still very popular for festival celebrations.

The other two inventions from ancient China are printing and paper. The first book to be printed was made in China. Paper was also first invented in China in the Han Dynasty. Before it was invented, words were engraved on various natural materials such as tortoise shells. For Chinese calligraphy, paper is one of the "Four Treasures" along with the writing brush, ink slab, and ink stick.

Useful expressions

你几点上课？	Nǐ jǐ diǎn shàng kè?	When does your class start?
你几点下课？	Nǐ jǐ diǎn xià kè?	When does your class end?
今天你有几节课？	Jīntiān nǐ yǒu jǐ jié kè?	How many hours of class do you have today?
今天晚上你有没有时间？	Jīntiān wǎnshang nǐ yǒu méiyǒu shíjiān?	Do you have time tonight?

Unit 8
School (II) 学校(二)

In this unit you will learn:

- how to give more information about people you know
- how to describe more about your school and library
- how to talk about your school, including lessons, subjects and timetable

Task 1　校长会说中国话

校	xiào	school
长	zhǎng	head, chief
来	lái	come
回	huí	return
说	shuō	speak, say
会	huì	can, will

Ex. 8.1 Listen to the recording carefully.

这是我的学校。这个人是我的校长。她是英国东北人。她姓小，英文是Small。我们都叫她小校长。

小校长今年四十五岁，她有一个女儿，今年十九岁，是一个大学

生。校长每天早上很早来学校，每天晚上六点半回家。

小校长也是我们的英文老师。她很喜欢学外文，也爱说外国话。日文、中国话她都会说。校长很爱学生，学生也都很喜欢她。

Ex. 8.2　Choose the right English meanings to fill in the blanks.

school	northeast	headmaster/ mistress	return
go (back) home	come	go	can, will
speak, say	can speak	southwest	
foreign country	foreign language	speech, sayings, language	
Chinese language	Japanese language	go (back) to one's home country	

1.	xiǎo	校		school
2.	xuéxiào	学校		
3.	zhǎng	长		head, chief
4.	xiǎozhǎng	校长		
5.	lái	来		
6.	qù	去		
7.	huí	回		
8.	huí jiā	回家		
9.	huí guó	回国		
10.	dōngběi	东北		
11.	xīnán	西南		
12.	shuō	说		
13.	huà	话		
14.	wàiguó	外国		
15.	wàiguóhuà	外国话		
16.	Zhōngguóhuà	中国话		
17.	Rìwén	日文		
18.	huì	会		
19.	huì shuō	会说		

Ex. 8.3　Listen to the wordlist and check your answers.

Unit 8
School (II) 学校(二)

Ex. 8.4 Read the text again and answer the questions based on the text in Chinese.

1. 这个人是谁?
2. 她姓什么?
3. 她是哪儿人?
4. 她喜欢学什么?
5. 她会说外国话吗?
6. 她每天几点回家?
7. 学生喜不喜欢她?

Grammar Notes   Position of time words

In Chinese, time words are placed before the verb. Look at the following sentences and pay attention to the position of the time words.

 The headmaster comes to school <u>in the morning every day</u>.
校长<u>每天早上</u>来学校。
Mother returns home at <u>6:30</u>.
妈妈<u>六点半</u>回家。
The students have classes <u>tomorrow morning</u>.
学生<u>明天上午</u>有课。

Ex. 8.5 Insert the time words into the right places.

1. 我喝英国茶。   (下午)

2. 学生来学校。   (早上八点半)

3. 他们不上课。   (现在)

4. 爸爸不吃中国饭。   (星期六)

5. 我家没有狗。   (去年)

Ex. 8.6 Character practice. Copy each character 4 times in the boxes provided.

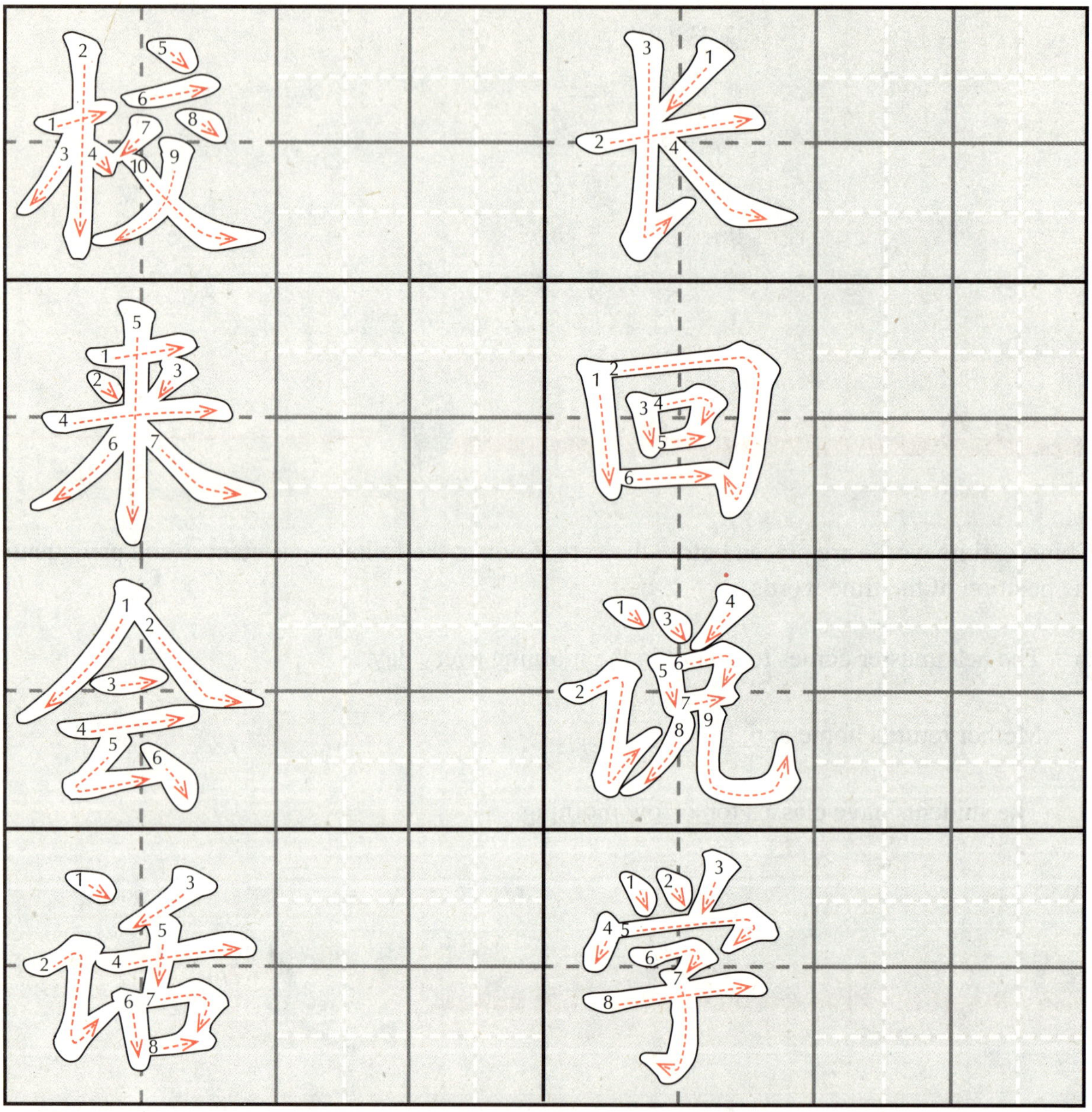

校			长		
来			回		
会			说		
话			学		

Ex. 8.7 Homework. Make up sentences by using the words/phrases provided, and then translate them into English.

1. 会　和　英文　说　我　中文　_____

2. 回家　下午　我的　每天　校长　五点半　_____

3. 是　这　你　的　吗　时间表　_____

Unit 8
School (II) 学校(二)

Task 2　教数学的是高老师

教	jiāo	teach
高	gāo	tall, high
先	xiān	first, precede
太	tài	great, too
起	qǐ	a group, get up
可	kě	but; may, can

Ex. 8.8　Listen to the recording carefully.

　　这三个人都是我的老师。教数学的是高先生。教英文的是马太太。高先生很高。马太太不高。高先生和马太太都是英国人。这个中国人是文小姐，她也是我的老师，教我们中文。

　　高先生，马太太和文小姐是好朋友。每个星期六他们都一起喝茶，一起吃饭。

　　高先生爱吃中国饭，可是不喜欢喝中国茶。文小姐喜欢喝英国茶，可是不爱吃英国饭。马太太哪国的饭都爱吃，什么茶都爱喝。

Ex. 8.9　Choose the right English meanings to fill the blanks.

first; precede	great, too	teach	but; may; can
a group; get up	student	but, however	tall, high; a surname
Mr.	Mrs.	Miss	horse; a surname
what	together		

1.	xiān	先	
2.	xiānsheng	先生	

3.	xuésheng	学生	
4.	jiāo	教	
5.	tài	太	
6.	tàitai	太太	
7.	xiǎojiě	小姐	
8.	gāo	高	
9.	mǎ	马	
10.	kě	可	
11.	kěshì	可是	
12.	qǐ	起	
13.	yìqǐ	一起	
14.	shénme	什么	

Ex. 8.10 Listen to the wordlist and check your answers.

Ex. 8.11 Read the text again and answer the following questions based on the text in Chinese.

1. 数学老师姓什么？
2. 英文老师姓什么？
3. 中文老师呢？
4. 谁很高？
5. 这三个老师星期几一起喝茶、吃饭？
6. 高先生爱吃什么？不爱喝什么？
7. 文小姐爱喝什么？不爱吃什么？
8. 马太太爱吃什么？爱喝什么？

Grammar Notes   Addressing people & 什么……都

1. When addressing people, Chinese always put surname before the title. Also professional title, such as teacher, 老师, is often used to address people.

   ▶   王先生   高太太   马小姐   文老师   王校长

2. 什么 means "what". It can also means "all kinds of" when it is used with 都. Look at the following sentences and pay attention to the sentence order.

Unit 8
School (II) 学校(二)

> Mrs. Ma loves to eat food.
> 马太太爱吃饭。
>
> Mrs. Ma loves to eat all kinds of food.
> 马太太什么饭都爱吃。
>
> Mrs. Ma doesn't like to drink any kind of tea.
> 马太太什么茶都不爱喝。

Ex. 8.12 Re-write the sentences with the "什么+Noun+都" structure.

例：马太太爱吃饭. ⇨ 马太太什么饭都爱吃.

1. 我喜欢喝茶。　　　_____
2. 这个人会说外文。　_____
3. 男老师不喜欢吃外国饭。_____

Grammar Notes 的 structure (1)

的 is a possessive marker. It can also be used to say the phrase: "the one/those that/ who…". Look at the following examples.

> my(friend)　　　　　我的(朋友)
> mine　　　　　　　我的
> today's　　　　　　今天的
> yesterday's　　　　 昨天的
> the big one　　　　 大的
> the small one　　　 小的
> the person who teaches mathematics　教我们数学的(人)
> The person who teaches us mathematics is Mr. Ma.　教我们数学的(人)是马先生。

Ex. 8.13 Read out the following expressions and translate them into English.

他的	哥哥的	姐姐的	弟弟的
高的	小的	好的	不好的
中国的	英国的	学校的	我家的
学数学的	有狗的	喝英国茶的	回家的
天天学外文的	不喜欢来学校的		

Ex. 8.14 Character practice. Copy each character 4 times in the boxes provided.

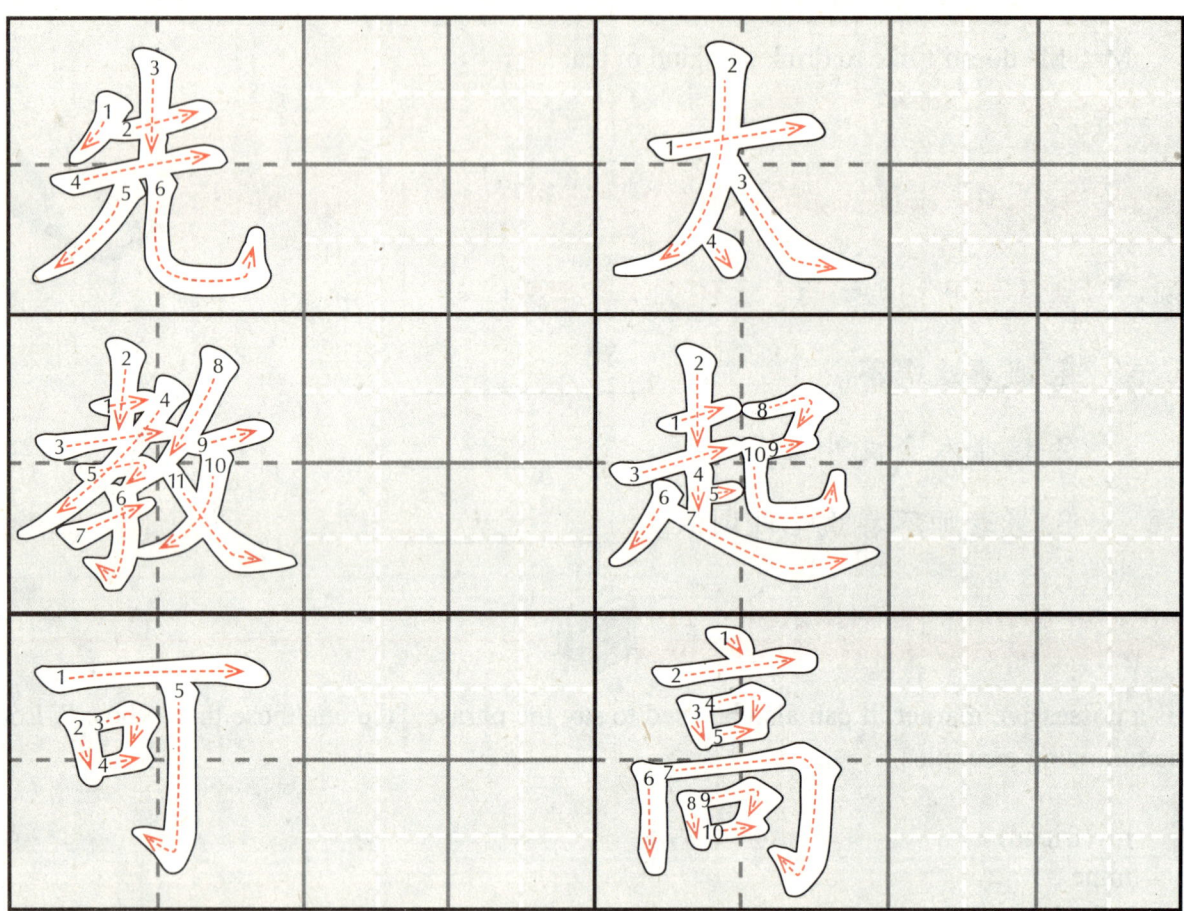

Ex. 8.15 Homework. Merge the following two sentences in each group into ONE sentence, using the 的 structure you have learnt.

例： He loves to drink tea.+ He is my father. =爱喝茶的(人)是我爸爸。

1. He loves to eat Chinese food.
   He is my elder brother. _____
2. She can speak Chinese.
   She is my headmistress. _____
3. She has two dogs.
   She is my very good friend. _____

Unit 8
School (II) 学校(二)

Task 3　学校有一个新图书馆

图	tú	picture, map
书	shū	book
馆	guǎn	hall
新	xīn	new
看	kàn	read, see, look, watch

Ex. 8.16　Listen to the recording and repeat.

这是我的学校。学校很大，有两个图书馆。一个老的，一个新的。老图书馆有很多老书，只有英文书，没有外文书。新图书馆很好，也很大。新图书馆有很多新书，有英文书，也有外文书。

每天下午图书馆都有很多人。不上课的学生都喜欢来图书馆看书。我喜欢去图书馆看外文书，我爱看新来的外文书。

Ex. 8.17　Choose the right English meanings to fill in the blanks.

new	picture, map	hall, gallery	read book(s)
old book(s)	new book(s)	library	newly arrived
maps and books		book(s)	restaurant
foreign language book(s)		read, see, look, watch	

| 1. | xīn | 新 | |

2.	xīn lái	新来的	
3.	shū	书	
4.	xīn shū	新书	
5.	lǎo shū	老书	
6.	wàiwén shū	外文书	
7.	tú	图	
8.	túshū	图书	
9.	guǎn	馆	
10.	túshūguǎn	图书馆	
11.	fànguǎn	饭馆	
12.	kàn	看	
13.	kàn shū	看书	

Ex. 8.18 Listen to the wordlist and check your answers.

Ex. 8.19 Read the text again and answer the following questions based on the text in Chinese.

1. 这个学校有没有图书馆?
2. 这个学校有几个图书馆?
3. 哪个图书馆只有英文书,没有外文书?
4. 哪个图书馆有英文书,也有外文书?
5. 图书馆下午人多不多?
6. 什么人来图书馆看书?

Grammar Notes 的 structure (2)

To say "the teacher who teaches us Chinese", you can simply use the 的 structure. Start from "teach us Chinese" first, then say "teacher". The important thing is to remember to put 的 in between.

教我们中文+的+老师
学中文+的+学生

Unit 8
School (II) 学校(二)

Ex. 8.20 Make up phrases by using the grammar notes and the words provided. Can you translate them into English?

学校+的+时间表 ⇨ 学校的时间表

图书馆	书
好看	人
姓王	老师
说中文	校长
看书	王小姐
不上课	学生
喜欢中文	马先生
爱吃中国饭	文太太
来中国	朋友
说英文	国家(country)

Ex. 8.21 Character practice. Copy each character 4 times in the boxes provided.

新 看
图 书
馆 饭

121

Ex. 8.22 Homework. Choose appropriate verbs to fill in the blanks. Then translate the sentences into English.

说   教   吃   学   喝   上   看

1. 王老师＿＿＿数学。　　　　＿＿＿＿＿＿＿＿＿＿＿＿＿＿＿

2. 学生喜欢＿＿＿化学。　　　＿＿＿＿＿＿＿＿＿＿＿＿＿＿＿

3. 妈妈不＿＿＿书。　　　　　＿＿＿＿＿＿＿＿＿＿＿＿＿＿＿

4. 爸爸天天早上＿＿＿英国茶。＿＿＿＿＿＿＿＿＿＿＿＿＿＿＿

5. 星期六下午不＿＿＿课。　　＿＿＿＿＿＿＿＿＿＿＿＿＿＿＿

6. 我的校长会＿＿＿外国话。　＿＿＿＿＿＿＿＿＿＿＿＿＿＿＿

7. 他和朋友们一起＿＿＿中国饭。＿＿＿＿＿＿＿＿＿＿＿＿＿＿

Culture factor

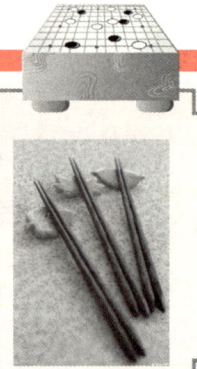

Anyone who has ever been to a Chinese restaurant knows that you have to use chopsticks rather than a knife and fork. Chopsticks were invented over 3,000 years ago. Chopsticks can be made out of many different materials. Normally they are made from wood or bamboo, but other materials can also be used for making chopsticks, such as silver and ivory.

Useful expressions

谁教你们数学？	Shéi jiāo nǐmen shùxué?	Who teaches you Math?
你去不去图书馆？	Nǐ qù bu qù túshūguǎn?	Do you go to the library?
我们一起去图书馆吧！	Wǒmen yìqǐ qù túshūguǎn ba!	Let's go to the library together!

Unit 9

Hobbies 爱好

In this unit you will learn:
- how to say your favourite sports
- how to talk about your other interests
- how to talk about your leisure time activities

Task 1 我最喜欢的运动是打球

运	yùn	revolve
动	dòng	move
最	zuì	the most/-est
打	dǎ	play, fight, do, strike
球	qiú	ball
网	wǎng	net, web
篮	lán	basket

Ex. 9.1 Listen to the recording and repeat.

你们好！我叫高小明，我今年十五岁。我的爱好是运动。什么运动我都喜欢。我最喜欢的运动是打球。

什么球我都喜欢打。我最喜欢打网球。我每个星期打两天网球。我和哥哥一起打网球。我也爱打篮球，每个星期三和星期六下午，我都和朋友一起打篮球。

Ex. 9.2 Choose the right English meanings to fill in the blanks.

```
move              play, fight, do, strike    ball       net, web
sports            love                       good       tennis
hobby             basketball                 basket     play ball games
the most / -est
```

1.	ài	爱	
2.	hǎo	好	
3.	àihǎo	爱好	
4.	yùn	运	revolve
5.	dòng	动	
6.	yùndòng	运动	
7.	zuì	最	
8.	dǎ	打	
9.	qiú	球	
10.	dǎ qiú	打球	
11.	wǎng	网	
12.	wǎngqiú	网球	
13.	lánqiú	篮球	
14.	lánzi	篮子	

Ex. 9.3 Listen to the wordlist and check your answers.

Ex. 9.4 Read the text again, then answer the following questions based on the text in Chinese.

1. 小明今年十几岁?
2. 小明的爱好是什么?
3. 他最喜欢什么运动?
4. 小明一个星期打几天网球?
5. 小明和谁一起打网球?
6. 小明星期三和星期六打什么球? 他和谁一起打?

Unit 9
Hobbies 爱好

Ex. 9.5 Extra vocabulary – more sports to play! Pay attention to the verb "to play", as it varies depending on the type of game.

(dǎ) páiqiú	(打) 排球	(play) volleyball
(dǎ) pīngpāngqiú	(打) 乒乓球	(play) table tennis
(dǎ) yǔmáoqiú	(打) 羽毛球	(play) badminton
(dǎ) gǎnlǎnqiú	(打) 橄榄球	(play) rugby
yóu yǒng	游 泳	swim
pǎo bù	跑 步	run
(tī) zúqiú	(踢) 足球	(play) football

Ex. 9.6 Pair work. Write down your most and least favourite subjects and sports. Exchange information with your partner by asking the following questions.

例：

你最喜欢什么课? 你最喜欢什么运动?
你最不喜欢什么课? 你最不喜欢什么运动?

                我   我的朋友

最喜欢的课	最喜欢的运动	最喜欢的课	最喜欢的运动
最不喜欢的课	最不喜欢的运动	最不喜欢的课	最不喜欢的运动

Ex. 9.7 Character practice. Copy each character 4 times in the boxes provided.

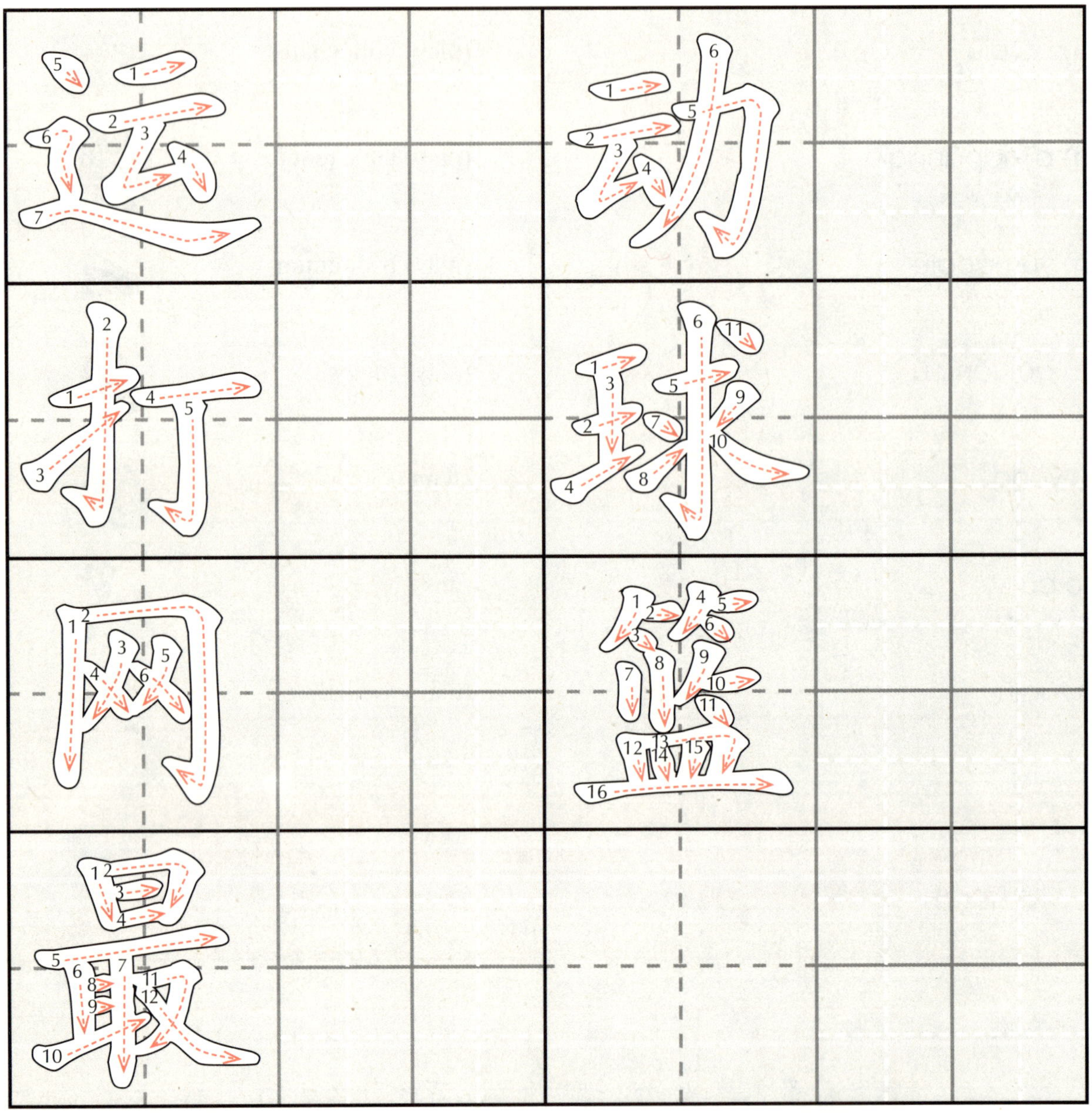

运 动
打 球
网 篮
最

Ex. 9.8 Homework. Translate the sentences below into Chinese using the words provided.

1. My favourite sport is tennis.

最喜欢的　是　网球　运动　我

Unit 9
Hobbies 爱好

2. I play tennis three days every week.

星期　　每个　　打　　三天　　我　　网球

3. I play basketball with my friends every Saturday afternoon at 2:30.

星期六　我　篮球　每个　下午　两点半　和朋友　一起　打

Task 2　学生没有时间看电视

视	shì	vision
到	dào	arrive; till
因	yīn	cause, reason
为	wèi	for; on account of
所	suǒ	that which; all that
以	yǐ	give cause; consider
常	cháng	frequently; normal; a surname

Ex. 9.9　Listen to the recording and repeat.

　　我是文月美，今年十四岁。我的爱好是看书和看电视。我什么书都喜欢看。新书、老书、英文书和中文书，我都爱看。我最爱看的书是小说，我喜欢一个人在家看小说。

　　我也很爱看电视。可是星期一到星期五我不看电视。为什么？因为我是学生，天天都上课，所以，没有时间看电视。我可以看电视的时间是星期六晚上和星期天，我常常和妹妹一起看电视。

Ex. 9.10   Choose the right English meanings to fill in the blanks.

```
electricity      television          till; arrive              be in/at/on
at home          often               frequently; a surname     may
watch TV         speak, say          therefore                 novel
why              read, see, watch    because
```

1.	zài	在	
2.	zài jiā	在家	
3.	shuō	说	
4.	xiǎoshuō	小说	
5.	kàn	看	
6.	diàn	电	
7.	shì	视	vision
8.	diànshì	电视	
9.	kàn diànshì	看电视	
10.	dào	到	
11.	yīn	因	cause, reason
12.	wèi	为	for; on account of
13.	yīnwèi	因为	
14.	wèishénme	为什么	
15.	suǒ	所	that which; all that
16.	yǐ	以	give cause; consider
17.	suǒyǐ	所以	
18.	kěyǐ	可以	
19.	cháng	常	
20.	chángcháng	常常	

Ex. 9.11   Listen to the wordlist and check your answers.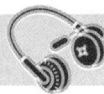

128

Unit 9
Hobbies 爱好

Ex. 9.12 Read the text again, then answer the following questions based on the text in Chinese.

1. 月美有什么爱好?
2. 她喜不喜欢看书?
3. 她喜欢看什么书?
4. 她喜欢和谁一起看小说?
5. 她喜欢在哪儿看书?
6. 星期一到星期五, 月美看不看电视? 为什么?
7. 月美星期天有时间看电视吗?
8. 她常常和谁一起看电视?

Grammar Notes　为什么，因为 & 因为……所以……

1. 为什么 (wèishénme) is a useful expression to ask reason(s) for something.

  > 你为什么学中文?
  > 你为什么爱吃中国饭?

2. 因为 (yīnwèi) is used to give reason(s). The following sentences give the reasons for the above two questions.

  > 因为我喜欢中国。
  > 因为中国饭很好吃 (hǎochī, delicious)。

3. 因为……所以…… (yīnwèi ... suǒyǐ ...) can be used together to give both reason and result.

  > 因为我喜欢中国，所以我学中文。
  > 因为中国饭很好吃，所以我喜欢吃中国饭。

Ex. 9.13 Line up the following reasons and results with the 因为……所以…… structure. Then read them out and translate them into English.

例：因为我喜欢中国，所以我学中国话。

新图书馆新书很多，　　　　　　　我也是中国人。

我喜欢看书，　　　　　　　　　他天天都有时间看电视。

弟弟不是学生，　　　　　　　　他每个星期六都打网球。

他的爱好是运动，　　　　　　　学生们都喜欢去新图书馆看书。

爸爸妈妈是中国人，　　　　　　我有很多书。

Grammar Notes 在

1. 在(zài) means "be in/at/on".

   妈妈在家。
   我在学校。
   老师在那儿。

2. "在+place+action" describes where an action happens. Please note that "在+place" precedes the action.

   I play basketball at school.　　　　　我在学校打篮球。
   The teacher eats at home.　　　　　　这个老师在家吃饭。
   Those two Chinese students read　　　那两个中国学生在图书馆看书。
     books at the library.

Unit 9
Hobbies 爱好

Ex. 9.14 Character practice. Copy each character 4 times in the boxes provided.

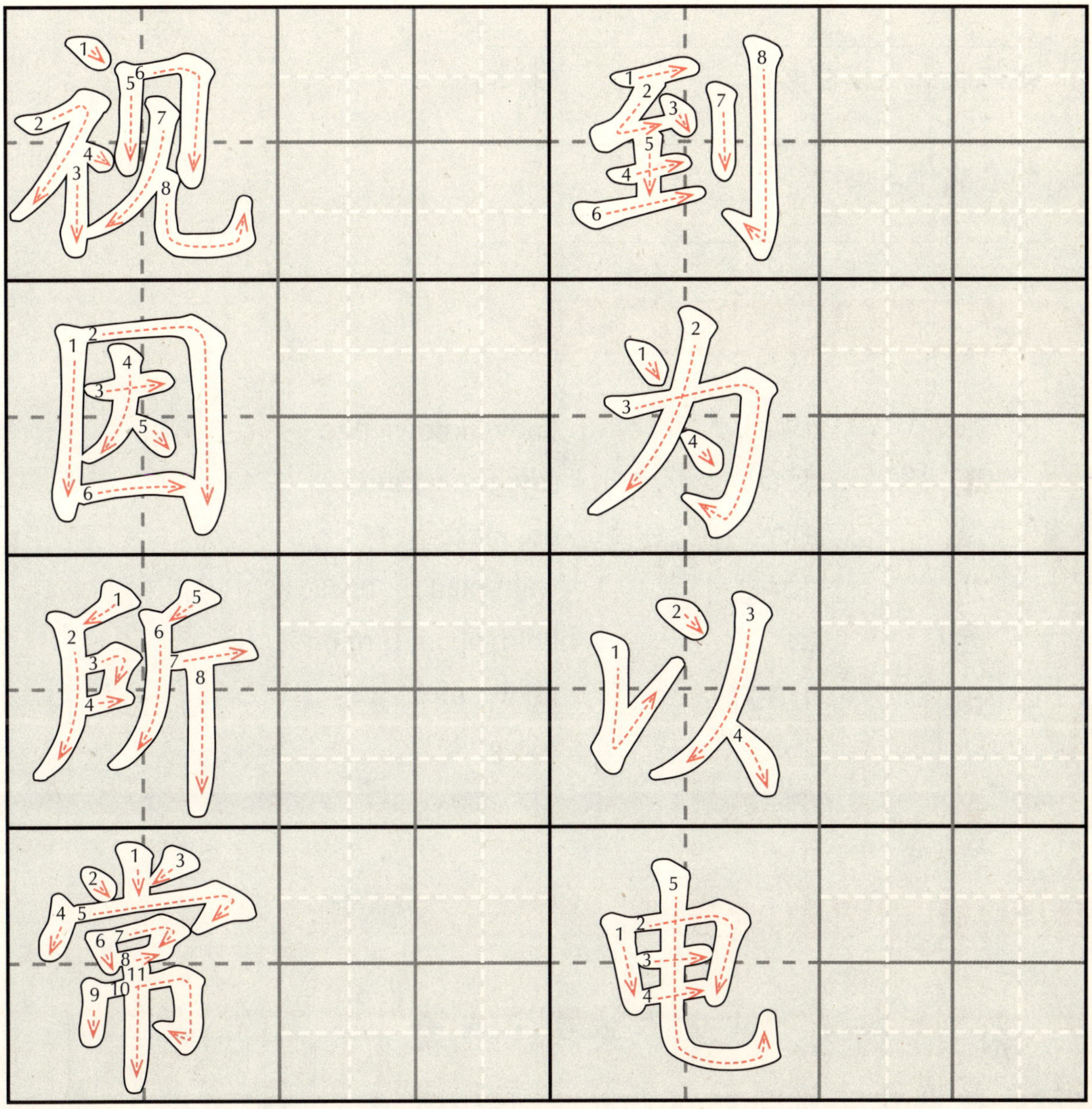

视			到		
因			为		
所			以		
常			电		

Ex. 9.15 Homework. Insert the given words into the correct places of the following sentences, then write them down and translate into English.

1. 我是中学生，没时间看电视。　　（因为……所以……）

_____

2. 妹妹喜欢看电视。　　　　　　　(在家)
_____

3. 男学生爱打篮球。　　　　　　　(都)
_____

4. 姐姐晚上在家看电视。　　　　　(常常)
_____

5. 你喜欢什么运动？　　　　　　　(最)
_____

Task 3　最好吃的中国饭

知	zhī	know; knowledge
道	dào	say; truth, path
做	zuò	do, make
想	xiǎng	want/plan to; miss
开	kāi	hold, open; turn on
请	qǐng	invite; please
给	gěi	for; give

Ex. 9.16　Listen to the recording and repeat.

我是王新文。我家在英国。我爱吃，最喜欢吃好吃的东西——不知道这是不是一个爱好？

我的爸爸妈妈都喜欢做饭。妈妈做饭很好吃。她会做英国饭，也会做中国饭。我爸爸也常常在家做饭，可是他做的饭很不好吃！所

Unit 9
Hobbies 爱好

以，我们都爱吃妈妈做的饭，没人喜欢吃爸爸做的饭。

下个星期天是我十五岁的生日，我想在家开一个生日会，请我的朋友来吃饭。妈妈说："我给你们做最好吃的中国饭！"

Ex. 9.17 Choose the right English meanings to fill in the blanks.

do, make   cook food   hold, open; turn on   for; give
east   invite; please   want/plan to; miss   west
birthday party delicious   hold a birthday party know
under, below   next Sunday   nobody

1.	dōng	东	
2.	xī	西	
3.	dōngxi	东西	thing
4.	zhī	知	know; knowledge
5.	dào	道	say; truth
6.	zhīdào	知道	
7.	hǎochī	好吃	
8.	méi rén	没人	
9.	xiǎng	想	
10.	qǐng	请	
11.	xià	下	
12.	xià gè Xīngqītiān	下个星期天	
13.	huì	会	meeting; can, will
14.	shēngrìhuì	生日会	
15.	kāi	开	
16.	kāi shēngrìhuì	开生日会	
17.	zuò	做	
18.	zuò fàn	做饭	
19.	gěi	给	

Ex. 9.18 Listen to the wordlist and check your answers.

Ex. 9.19 Read the text again, then answer the following questions based on the text in Chinese.

1. 王新文家在哪儿?
2. 他的爱好是什么?
3. 他家谁做饭?
4. 他家谁做饭好吃? 谁做饭不好吃?
5. 王新文现在多大?
6. 下个星期天王新文想做什么? 为什么?
7. 他想请谁?
8. 谁给他们做饭?

Grammar Notes   Adjective scales & 给

1. Scales

| 最喜欢 | 很喜欢 | 喜欢 | 不太喜欢 | 不喜欢 | 很不喜欢 |
| 最好 | 很好 | 好 | 不太好 | 不好 | 很不好 |

2. 给 (gěi) means "to give". It is also used to say "for sb.", "on one's behalf".

I give him Chinese tea.　　　　　　我给他中国茶。
Mother cooks for us.　　　　　　　妈妈给我们做饭。

Ex. 9.20 Can you use the scale of 喜欢 to express how you feel about the following things? Write down two sentences after saying them.

最喜欢	很喜欢	喜欢	不太喜欢	不喜欢	很不喜欢
数学	中国饭	学校	茶	运动	
看书	校长	看电视	打网球	学中文	

_____

_____

Unit 9
Hobbies 爱好

Ex. 9.21 Character practice. Copy each character 4 times in the boxes provided.

想			做		
知			道		
请			给		
开			会		

Ex. 9.22 Homework. Translate the following sentences into Chinese.

1. I want to hold a birthday party at home. _____
2. I want to hold a birthday party this Sunday. _____
3. Who wants to cook tonight? _____
4. I don't know who cooks for us. _____
5. Please give the teacher a call tonight. (give a call: 打[一个]电话)
   _____

135

Culture factor

What surprises most westerners when they go to China is to see men and women over 80 in the parks at 6 o'clock in the morning practising Taichi and Qigong. Even in school, exercise is a very important part of the curriculum. Children are taught sports such as football, basketball, tennis, and, of course, table tennis. In China many people also practise martial arts, or kungfu. Martial arts in China have different styles in the north and south.

Useful expressions

请问……	Qǐngwèn ...	Please may I ask…
你喜欢运动吗?	Nǐ xǐhuan yùndòng ma?	Do you like sports?
你喜欢什么运动?	Nǐ xǐhuan shénme yùndòng?	Which sport do you like?
你会不会打网球?	Nǐ huì bu huì dǎ wǎngqiú?	Can you play tennis?

Unit 10
Daily Routine 日常生活

In this unit you will learn:
- daily routines
- time expressions
- how to talk about how you have learned Chinese

Task 1   很忙的中学生

总	zǒng	anyway; general, main
忙	máng	busy
床	chuáng	bed
后	hòu	afterwards, behind
放	fàng	release, put

Ex. 10.1   Listen to the recording and repeat.

我叫高小南，我是一个中学生。大家都知道，中学生总是很忙。星期一到星期五，我天天都很忙。

这是我每天的时间表——早上七点半起床，起床以后吃早饭。早饭以后，八点十分去学校上课。在学校，我们上午上三个小时的课。中午十二点我们在学

7：30	起床
7：30—8：10	吃早饭
8：10	去学校
9：00—12：00	上课
12：00—13：00	吃午饭
13：00—15：00	上课
15：00	学校放学
15：00—16：30	和朋友打篮球
16：30	回家

校吃午饭。下午我们只上两个小时的课。学校下午三点放学。

放学以后,我常常在学校和朋友打一会儿篮球。我每天四点半回家。

Ex. 10.2   Choose the right English meanings to fill in the blanks.

busy	bed	get up; group	get up (get out of bed)
everyone	always	go to	attend class
after	release, put	afterwards; in the future	
finish a class	attend school	release from (finish) school	

1.	dàjiā	大家	
2.	zǒng	总	anyway; general, main
3.	zǒngshì	总是	
4.	máng	忙	
5.	qù	去	
6.	chuáng	床	
7.	qǐ	起	
8.	qǐ chuáng	起床	
9.	hòu	后	
10.	yǐhòu	以后	
11.	shàng kè	上课	
12.	xià kè	下课	
13.	shàng xué	上学	
14.	fàng	放	
15.	fàng xué	放学	
16.	yíhuìr	一会儿	(for) a while

Ex. 10.3   Listen to the wordlist and check your answers.

138

Unit 10
Daily Routine 日常生活

Ex. 10.4 Read the text again, then answer the following questions based on the text in Chinese.

1. 高小南是不是中学生？
2. 他星期几到星期几上课？
3. 他每天早上几点起床？
4. 他几点去学校上课？
5. 他上午上几个小时的课？下午呢？
6. 学校几点放学？
7. 放学以后，他做什么？
8. 他每天几点回家？

Grammar Notes 都，总是 & time expression

1. "Everyone knows" in Chinese is 大家都知道 or 人人都知道 or 每个人都知道. The important thing is: don't forget to use 都 before the verb.

> 人人都知道他是中国人。
> 大家都知道中国饭好吃。
> 每个人都想学中文。

2. 总是 means "always".

> 中学生总是很忙。
> 他总是喜欢早起床。
> 他总是星期三下午打网球。

3. How to express the "duration of time"?

a while	一会儿	half an hour	半个小时
two hours	两个小时	twelve days	十二天
three weeks	三个星期	five months	五个月
six years	六年		

How do you say "to play basketball for a while"? Simply place the time duration between the verb and activities. Generally, 的 is needed before the activities.

> 打篮球　　　打一会儿篮球
> 看电视　　　看半个小时的电视
> 上课　　　　上一个小时的课

Ex. 10.5 Rewrite the following sentences with the words given in brackets, then say their meanings.

1. 我知道他会说中文。　　　　(英国话) _____
2. 每个人都喜欢那个女学生。　(男学生) _____
3. 这儿家家都有电视。　　　　(人人)　 _____
4. 他常常做好吃的饭。　　　　(总是)　 _____
5. 中学生很忙。　　　　　　　(不)　　 _____

Ex. 10.6 Character practice. Copy each character 4 times in the boxes provided.

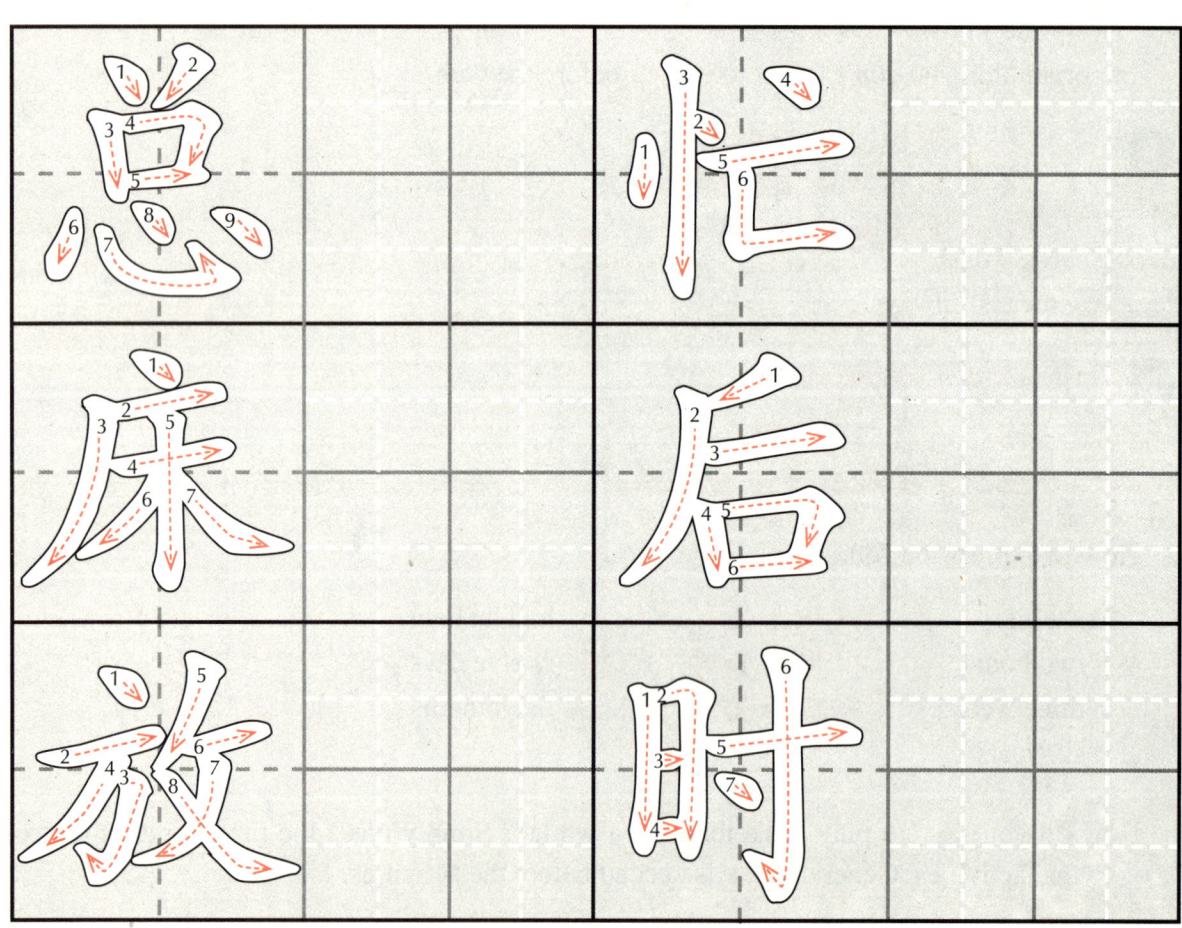

Unit 10
Daily Routine 日常生活

Ex. 10.7 Homework. Insert the time length provided into the right places of the following sentences. Don't forget to add 的 in front of the activities.

1. 王老师想教数学。 (两年) _____
2. 弟弟天天晚上看电视。 (一个半小时) _____
3. 我们每个星期上英文课。 (三个小时) _____
4. 我七月去北京学中文。 (一个月) _____
5. 我每天下午在图书馆看书。(一个小时) _____

Task 2   告诉爸爸妈妈学校的事情

候	hòu	timing, weather; wait
告	gào	tell, sue
诉	sù	tell; go to court
事	shì	matter, fact, event
情	qíng	affection, feeling
完	wán	finish, complete

Ex. 10.8   Listen to the recording and repeat.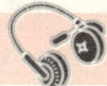

我是小天。我每天四点半放学。放学回家以后，我总是和妈妈一起做饭。爸爸回家以后，我们一起吃晚饭。有时候七点吃饭，有时候七点半吃饭。

吃饭的时候，我喜欢和爸爸妈妈说话。我告诉他们一点儿学校的事情：今天上什么课，学校的老师

好不好，我和朋友一起做什么……我和爸爸妈妈总是有很多话说。吃完晚饭以后，我看书，爸爸和妈妈看电视。

Ex. 10.9 Choose the right English meanings to fill in the blanks.

finish, complete	issue, matter	time
tell	speak, say	talk
when...; while...	when	sometimes
a tiny amount; o'clock	a little; some	

1.	shí	时	time
2.	hòu	候	timing, weather; wait
3.	shíhou	时候	
4.	yǒushíhou	有时候	
5.	...de shíhou	……的时候	
6.	shénme shíhou	什么时候	
7.	shuō	说	
8.	huà	话	speech, talk; story, discussion
9.	shuō huà	说话	
10.	gào	告	tell, sue
11.	sù	诉	tell; go to court
12.	gàosu	告诉	
13.	shì	事	matter, fact, event
14.	qíng	情	affection, feeling
15.	shìqing	事情	
16.	diǎn	点	
17.	yìdiǎnr	一点儿	
18.	wán	完	

Ex. 10.10 Listen to the wordlist and check your answers.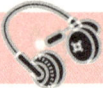

Ex. 10.11 Read the text again, then answer the following questions based on the text in Chinese.

1. 小天每天几点放学？
2. 放学回家以后，她做什么？

Unit 10
Daily Routine 日常生活

3. 她们家几点吃晚饭?
4. 小天吃饭的时候,告诉爸爸妈妈什么?
5. 吃完晚饭以后,爸爸妈妈做什么?
6. 吃完晚饭以后,小天做什么?

Grammar Notes ……的时候 & 一点儿

1. "When…" in Chinese is ……的时候(... de shíhou). This is a very useful expression.

   ▶ When I was little…   我小的时候……
   When they were in China… 他们在中国的时候……

2. 一点儿(yìdiǎnr) means "a little bit, a little". Mainly used for uncountable nouns.

   ▶ Give me a little time.   给我一点儿时间。
   Give me a little water.   给我一点儿水。
   Give me a little water to drink.   给我一点儿水喝。
   He can speak a little Chinese.   他会说一点儿中文。

Ex. 10.12 Line up the following expressions with their English meanings.

我小的时候   when (sb.) watches TV

我十岁的时候   when (sb.) returns home

三月的时候   when (sb.) eats a meal

二零零三年的时候   when I was little

看电视的时候   when I was ten years old

吃饭的时候   when (it is in) March

回家的时候   when (sb.) doesn't want to play tennis

不想打网球的时候   when (it is in the) year 2003

143

Ex. 10.13　Character practice. Copy each character 4 times in the boxes provided.

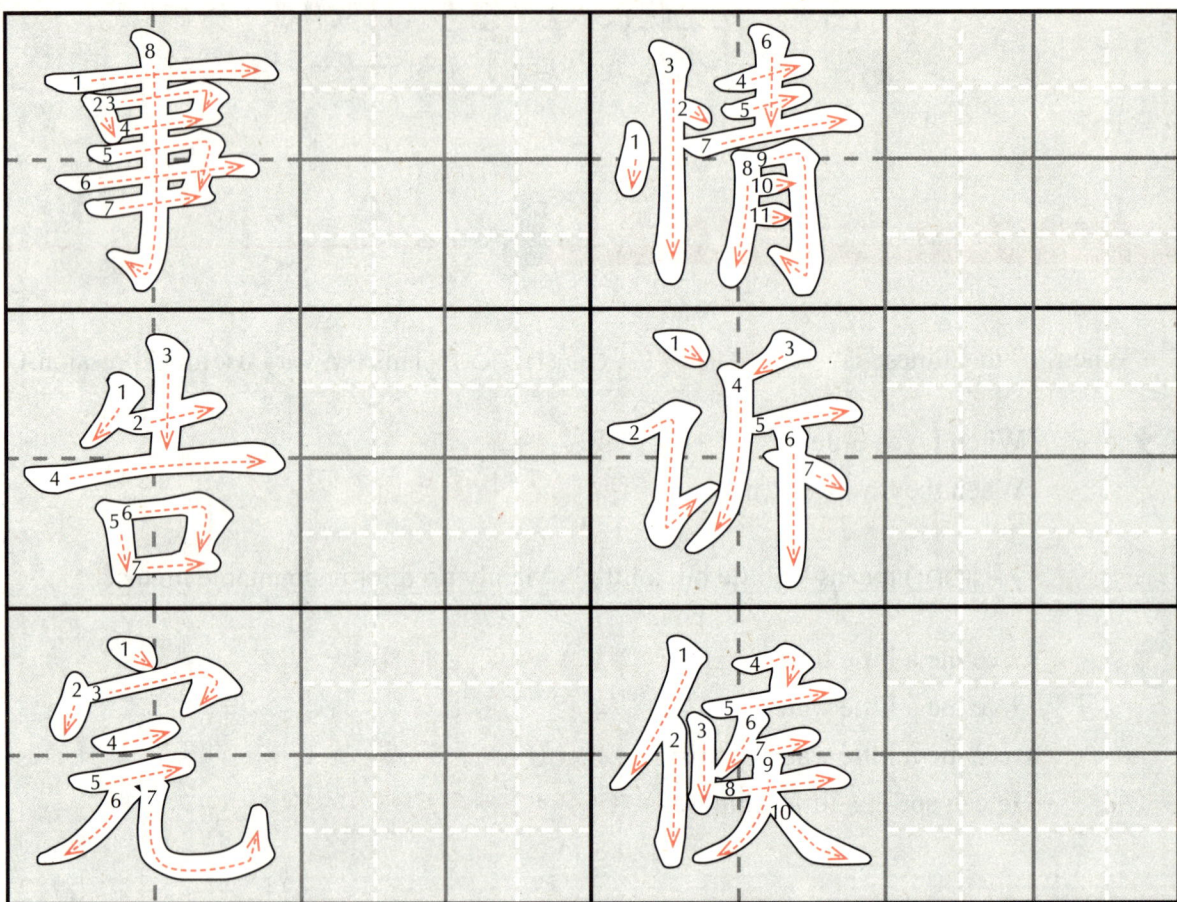

Ex. 10.14　Homework. Translate the following sentences into Chinese.

1. When I was 10 years old, I didn't like to read (books).
   _____

2. When it is 8 o'clock, I go to school.
   _____

3. When we eat supper, we don't watch TV.
   _____

4. While mother is cooking, my younger sister and I read books.
   _____

5. Give him a little water to drink.
   _____

Unit 10
Daily Routine 日常生活

Task 3 你应该学一点儿中文

能	néng	can; ability, power, energy
写	xiě	write
应	yīng	should; ought to
该	gāi	should; ought to
始	shǐ	a beginning
前	qián	in front of ; forward; preceding

Ex. 10.15　Listen to the recording and repeat.

我叫常天爱，今年十四岁。我家在英国，我妈妈是中国人，爸爸是英国人。我小的时候，会说一点儿中文，可是不能看，也不能写。妈妈总是说："你是半个中国人，你应该学一点儿中文！"

前年开始，我在学校学中文。每个星期我上三个小时的中文课。我有两个中文老师。以前是一个男老师，现在是一个女老师。两个老师都是中国人。新的女老师姓文，我知道她是南京人。她告诉我，她以前在北京大学学英文。她是一个很好的老师，我很喜欢她。

我很喜欢学中文，现在我能说中文，能看中文小说，也能写一点儿中文。

Ex. 10.16 Choose the right English meanings to fill in the blanks.

write	can; ability, power, energy	should; ought to
start (work)	the year before last	open; turn on
(an) hour	the day before yesterday	maybe, possible
may, can	Nanjing (a city name)	Peking University
but, however	afterward; in the future	in the past; before

1.	yīng	应	should
2.	gāi	该	ought to
3.	yīnggāi	应该	
4.	xiě	写	
5.	kāi	开	
6.	shǐ	始	a beginning
7.	kāishǐ	开始	
8.	qián	前	vs. 后 in front of; forward; preceding
9.	qiánnián	前年	
10.	qiántiān	前天	
11.	yǐqián	以前	
12.	yǐhòu	以后	
13.	Nánjīng	南京	
14.	Běijīng Dàxué	北京大学	
15.	néng	能	
16.	kěnéng	可能	
17.	kěshì	可是	
18.	kěyǐ	可以	
19.	xiǎoshí	小时	

Ex. 10.17 Listen to the wordlist and check your answers.

Ex. 10.18 Read the text again, then answer the following questions based on the text in Chinese.

1. 天爱今年多少岁?
2. 天爱是不是英国人?

Unit 10
Daily Routine 日常生活

3. 天爱小时候会说中文吗?
4. 天爱什么时候开始学中文?
5. 她有几个中文老师?
6. 女老师姓什么? 她是中国哪儿人?
7. 女老师以前在哪个大学上学? 她在大学学什么?
8. 女老师是不是一个好老师?
9. 现在天爱的中文好不好?

Grammar Notes   Modal verb

Modal verbs (auxiliaries) are used in front of verbs to show possibility, ability and related concepts. Look at the following examples and pay attention to the sentences with the modal verb 想(xiǎng).

她做中国饭。　　　　　她想做中国饭。
她不做中国饭。　　　　她不想做中国饭。
她做不做中国饭?　　　她想不想做中国饭?
她做中国饭吗?　　　　她想做中国饭吗?

Ex. 10.19 Here are some modal verbs that we have learnt throughout the book. Can you write down their English meanings?

能	néng	
可以	kěyǐ	
应该	yīnggāi	
喜欢	xǐhuan	
爱	ài	
想	xiǎng	
会	huì	

Grammar Notes   以前 & 以后

以前(yǐqián) means "before; in the past" and 以后(yǐhòu) means "after, afterwards; in the future". They may be used alone or combined with other expressions. Read out the following examples and translate them into English.

以前 　　　　　　　　　以后
九点以前 　　　　　　　九点以后
三天以前 　　　　　　　三天以后
五个月以前 　　　　　　五个月以后
十年以前 　　　　　　　十年以后

以前，我是小学生。现在，我是中学生。以后，我是大学生。

Ex. 10.20 Character practice. Copy each character 4 times in the boxes provided.

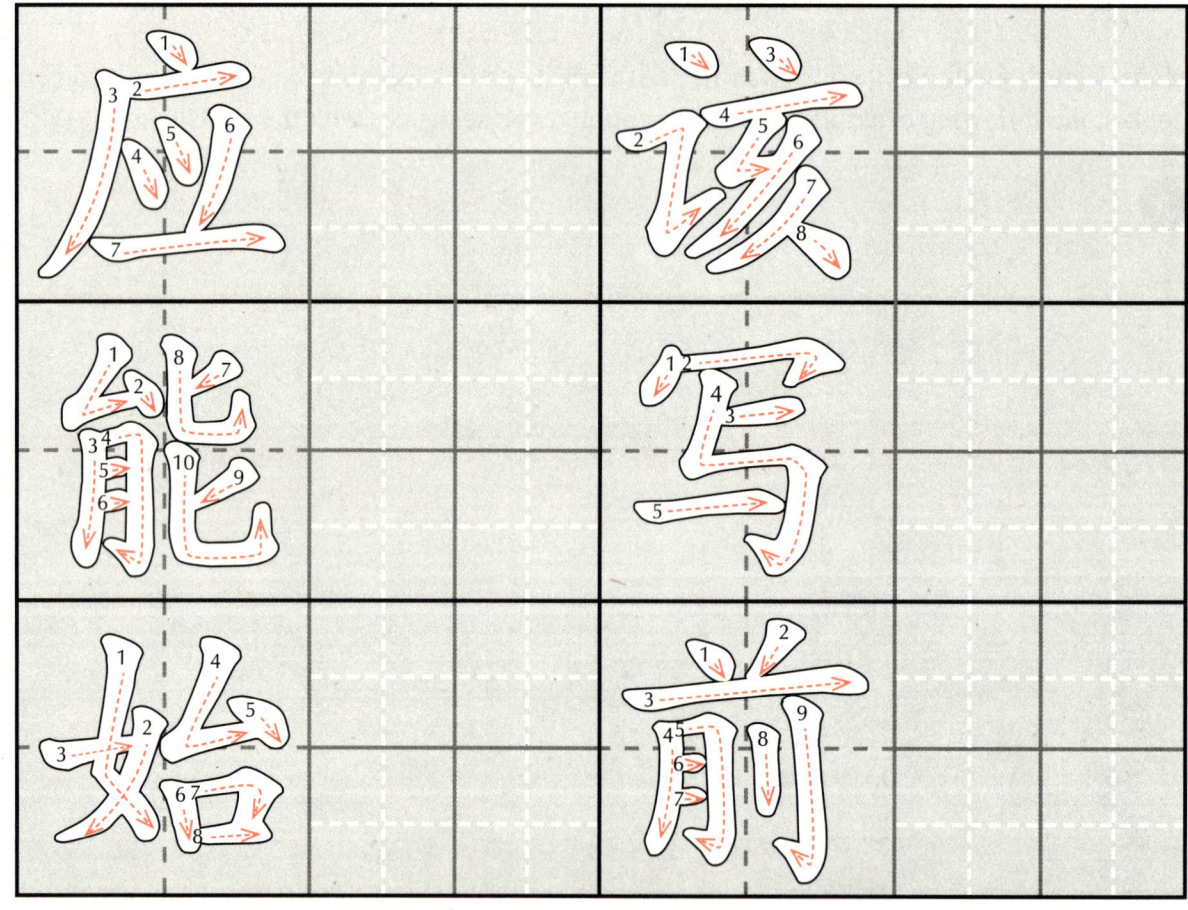

Ex. 10.21 Homework. Choose appropriate modal verbs to fill in the blanks. Some blanks have more than one option. Then translate your sentences into English.

爱　　想　　喜欢　　会　　能　　可以　　应该

1. 美国中学生＿＿＿＿＿＿＿打篮球。

Unit 10
Daily Routine 日常生活

2. 他_____说一点儿中文，你_____说中文吗？

3. 我爸爸妈妈是中国人，所以我_____学一点儿中文。

4. 你_____早一点儿(a bit earlier)回家。

5. 我朋友_____以后去中国学中文。

Culture factor

Red is considered a lucky colour in China. Because of this, all festivities and big occasions always have red banners, pictures, and people wearing red clothes. During weddings, for example, traditionally the bride would always wear a red dress, but nowadays, due to western influence, some brides choose a white dress to wear on their wedding day.

Useful expressions

我们认识一下，我是……	Wǒmen rènshi yí xià, wǒ shì…
	Let me introduce myself, I am…
我来介绍一下，这是……	Wǒ lái jièshao yí xià, zhè shì…
	Let me make introductions, this is…
我会说一点儿中文。	Wǒ huì shuō yì diǎnr Zhōngwén.
	I can speak a little Chinese.
祝你快乐！	Zhù nǐ kuàilè!
	Wish you happiness!
新年快乐！	Xīnnián kuàilè!
	Happy New Year!

Revision Unit 2

Poem with Numbers

乡村
Xiāngcūn

一去二三里，
Yí qù èr sān lǐ,
烟村四五家。
yān cūn sì wǔ jiā.
亭台六七座，
Tíng tái liù qī zuò,
八九十枝花。
bā jiǔ shí zhī huā.

Country Village
(Translated by Jonny Moses)

I once roamed alone for two or three miles,

till I saw four or five houses, their smoke through the bowers,

amidst six, seven pavilions I paused for awhile,

as time slipped away, beside eight nine ten or so flowers.

咏雪
Yǒng Xuě

一片二片三四片，
Yí piàn èr piàn sān sì piàn,

五六七八九十片，
wǔ liù qī bā jiǔ shí piàn.

千片万片无数片，
qiān piàn wàn piàn wúshù piàn,

飞入芦花总不见。
fēi rù lúhuā zǒng bú jiàn.

The Snow Chant
(Translated by Jonny Moses)

One falls, two fall,
three, four flakes,

Five, wait, eight now,
Nine, ten flakes,

Tens of thousands,
countless flakes,

Sieved through catkins,
the snow veil breaks.

Revision Unit 2

Character Review

1. Draw lines to link an upper part with a lower part. This will create a character that you know. Write them down in the boxes provided and their meanings.

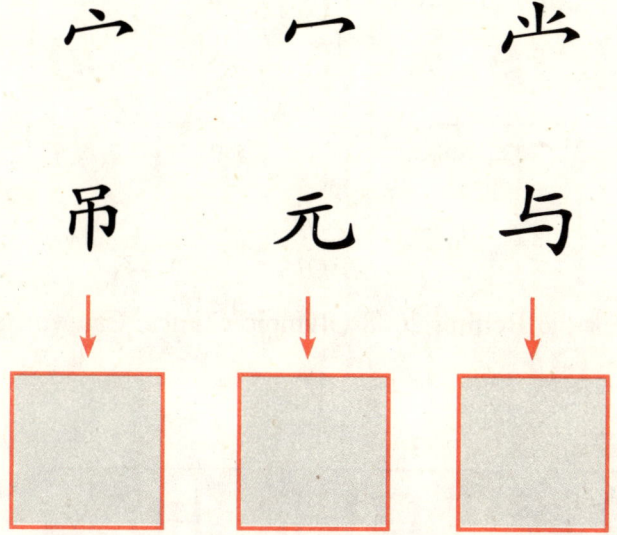

2. Here are more radicals. Write characters with the meanings provided.

亠			
head	capital	tall	
辶			
walk	road	this	
文→攵			
rap	teach	number	do
食→饣			
food	meal	restaurant	
囗			
enclosure	because	country	

151

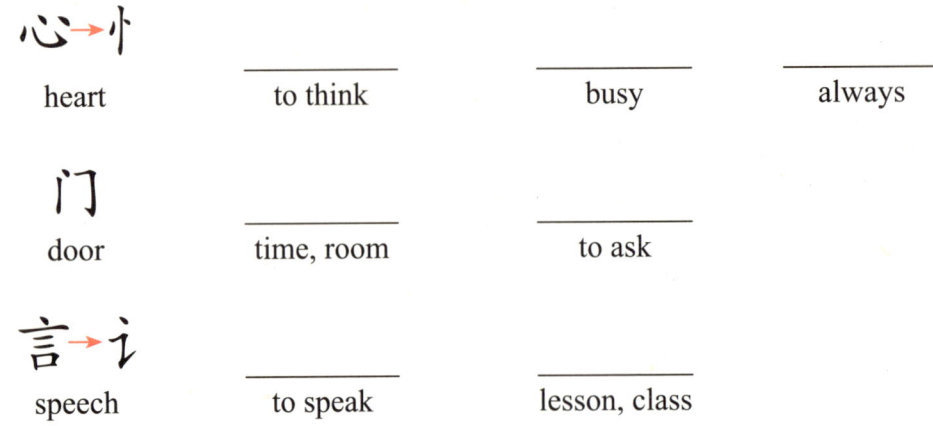

心→忄
heart   to think   busy   always

门
door   time, room   to ask

言→讠
speech   to speak   lesson, class

3. Here is an advertisement for the Beijing 2008 Olympic Games. Can you guess the sports that these characters stand for?

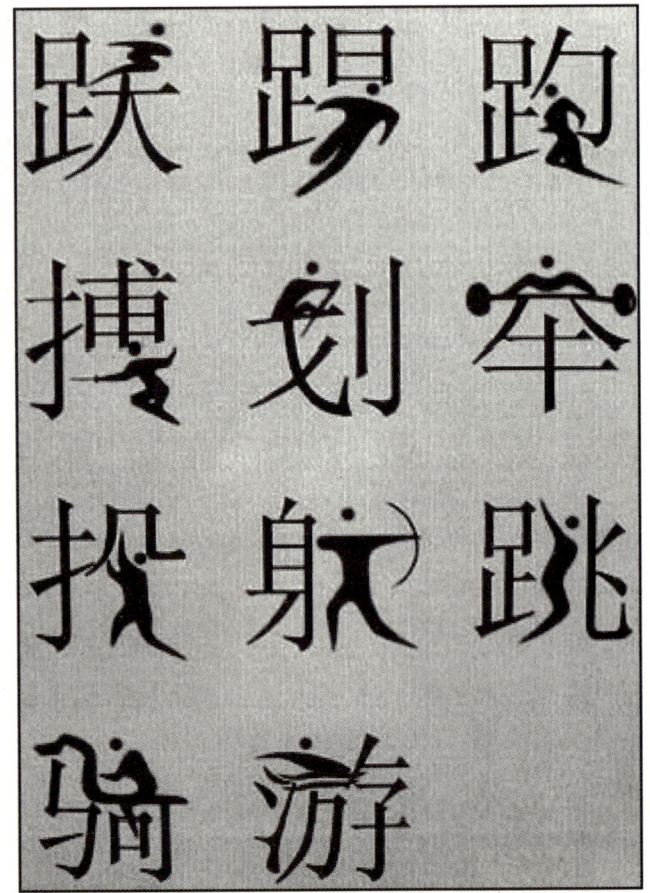

Revision Unit 2

4. Learning Chinese characters can be fun! Below you will find cartoons which represent Chinese characters that you have learnt in this book. Can you guess the meaning of each cartoon?

们　王　英　有　不　家

Progress Test 3 (Unit1T1- Unit6T3)

1. Translate the following words into English. (15%)

(1) 小 _____   姓 _____   马 _____   家 _____

(2) 日 _____   月 _____   明 _____   天 _____

(3) 好 _____   美 _____   叫 _____   很 _____

(4) 星期 _____   号 _____   年 _____   狗年 _____

(5) 五只羊 _____   四个弟弟 _____   六口人 _____   七月 _____

(6) 英国 _____   生日 _____   天天 _____   今天 _____

(7) 在 _____   问 _____   学 _____   去 _____

(8) 小老师 _____   老学生 _____   好朋友 _____   家人 _____

(9) 谁 _____   哪 _____   什么 _____   那 _____

(10) 喝茶 _____   现在 _____   北京 _____   中东 _____

(11) 早 _____   晚 _____   晚上 _____   中午 _____

(12) 东北 _____   西南 _____   南 _____   北 _____

(13) 去年	昨天	今年	明天
(14) 九月	一七七零年	星期六	两点半
(15) 少	多	几	多少

2. Translate the following sentences into English. (40%)

(1) 哪个电话是你的?

(2) 这个人不是英国人,也不是美国人。

(3) 那是什么?

(4) 她是哪国人?

(5) 哥哥爱喝中国茶,弟弟也喜欢喝中国茶。

(6) 爸爸有很多英国茶,他早上喝,晚上也喝。

(7) 我的好朋友叫英英,她有两个弟弟。

(8) 你的生日是九月十七日吗?

(9) 我问你,今年是二零零几年?去年呢?

(10) 小月的爸爸有一个英国电话。

(11) 这个女老师是好老师吗?

(12) 明天是几月几号?

(13) 北京在中国,东京不在中国。

(14) 小美的妈妈天天早上喝茶,晚上不喝。

(15) 这两个电话,一个是我的,一个是老师的,你喜欢哪个?

(16) 明年六月我去美国。

(17) 上个星期六是谁的生日?

(18) 我的朋友很多,有很多英国人,没有中国人。

(19) 学生问老师:"你喜欢狗吗?你有狗吗?"

(20) 现在是星期六下午四点半。

(21) 这个美国男老师的英国女朋友有三只很小的中国狗。

(22) 这个中国老师有多少个男学生?

(23) 我不是大学生,我只是一个中学生。

(24) 你爱喝什么茶?

(25) 那个中学老师有很多朋友。
_____

3. Translate the following passages into English. (10%)

(1) 我家有四口人,爸爸妈妈,我,妹妹。我的生日是十一月二十二日,是这个星期四。我妹妹叫东美,她的生日是八月二十六号。
_____
_____

(2) 我是一个中学生。我有很多老师,我也有很多朋友。我的好朋友叫大山,他是半个美国人,半个英国人。明天是星期天,也是大山的生日。我明天下午去大山家。
_____
_____
_____

4. Translate the following sentences into Chinese characters. (25%)

(1) What day is today?
(2) I am also Chinese.
(3) Who is your father's friend?
(4) I don't have telephone, how about you?
(5) How many days is a week?
(6) My teachers are my good friends.
(7) British people like to drink tea in the morning.
(8) Next Saturday is my birthday.
(9) China is very beautiful!
(10) That dog is not mine, this one is.

5. Answer the following questions with Chinese characters. (10%)

(1) Q: 你是美国人吗?
    A: _____

(2) Q: 你家谁是中学生?
    A: _____

(3) Q: 你有没有狗?
    A: _____

(4) Q: 你姓什么?
    A: _____

(5) Q: 现在几点?
    A: _____

Progress Test 4 (Unit1T1- Unit8T3)

1. Translate the following words into English. (15%)

(1) 说 _____   教 _____   吃 _____   喝 _____

(2) 看 _____   问 _____   学 _____   姓 _____

(3) 来 _____   去 _____   回 _____   有 _____

(4) 电话 _____   外文 _____   时间 _____   数学 _____

(5) 学校 _____   化学 _____   图书馆 _____   狗 _____

(6) 东西 _____   老师 _____   文学 _____   九百 _____

(7) 先生 _____   小姐 _____   学生 _____   太太 _____

(8) 可是 _____   很 _____   会 _____   也 _____

(9) 上课 _____   英国茶 _____   校长 _____   大家 _____

(10) 一起 _____   高 _____   新 _____   老 _____

(11) 东北 _____   西南 _____   南 _____   北 _____

(12) 点 _____   分 _____   半 _____   午 _____

(13) 去年 _____   昨天 _____   今年 _____   明天 _____

159

(14)　八月　　　一七七零年　　　星期六　　　两点半

(15)　小学　　　生日会　　　　大学生　　　下课

2. Translate the following sentences into English. (30%)

(1) 这个电话是你的吗?

(2) 那个老师是哪国人?

(3) 中国茶,英国茶我都喜欢。

(4) 他家天天都吃中国饭。

(5) 我的中学有五百多个英国学生,一百多个外国学生。

(6) 星期六我们只上半天课。

(7) 这是我的时间表,教英文的是文老师。

(8) 你明天上午有没有数学课?

(9) 高先生是老师吗? 他教什么课?

(10) 马太太什么饭都爱吃,什么茶都爱喝。

(11) 我的校长很爱学外文。

(12) 学校的新图书馆很好,有很多新书。
_____

(13) 爱去图书馆看书的学生是好学生。
_____

(14) 我下午三点半回家。
_____

(15) 我今年十五岁,是一个中学生。
_____

3. **Translate the following passages into English. (15%)**

(1) 这是我星期一的时间表。上午九点上课,中午十二点下课。十二点到一点吃午饭。学生们都在学校吃午饭。下午一点上课,四点下课。
_____
_____

(2) 我的中学在北京,叫北京美文中学。学校是一个新学校,不太大,只有四百多个学生,老师也不多,有四十个。我的数学老师、化学老师都是中国人,英文老师是一个四十多岁的美国女老师,她很好。
_____
_____
_____

(3) 我是半个英国人,半个中国人。我们家星期六晚上吃中国饭。人人都爱吃中国饭。早上我和爸爸喝英国茶,妈妈喝中国茶。妹妹今年十岁,她不喝茶,只喝水。
_____
_____
_____

4. Translate the following into Chinese characters. (30%)

(1) Everyone in my family loves tea.

(2) We eat Chinese food every Saturday evening.

(3) Do you like Math?

(4) What time is it now?

(5) Who doesn't have a dog?

(6) American doesn't like to drink tea.

(7) Today is Sunday.

(8) What is the surname of your Chemistry teacher?

(9) Do you have lessons on Fridays?

(10) What time do you attend Chinese class?

(11) My headmaster can speak foreign languages.

(12) The new library is (over) there.

(13) This is my book. That is my telephone.

(14) I eat Chinese food with my Chinese friends.
_____

(15) The male teacher goes back home at 5:30 everyday.
_____

5. Answer the following questions with Chinese characters. (10%)

(1) Q: 你有几个老师?
    A: _____

(2) Q: 你的学校有多少学生?
    A: _____

(3) Q: 你的学校有没有图书馆?
    A: _____

(4) Q: 星期六下午你上课吗?
    A: _____

(5) Q: 你喜欢中国茶吗?
    A: _____

End of book I Test (Unit1- Unit10)

1. Translate the following words into English. (15%)

(1)	说话	告诉	知道	喜欢
(2)	时间	网球	电视	数学
(3)	运动	上课	放学	做饭
(4)	可是	可以	可能	所以
(5)	看书	打球	回家	打球
(6)	事情	东西	老师	文学
(7)	起床	开始	先生	小姐
(8)	现在	以前	以后	时候
(9)	总是	一起	应该	因为
(10)	忙	完	高	新
(11)	写	最	教	给
(12)	东北	西南	南	北
(13)	去年	昨天	今年	明天

(14)　八月　　　　　一七七零年　　　　星期六　　　　两点半

(15)　时间表　　　　生日会　　　　　　校长　　　　　图书馆

2. Translate the following sentences into English. (30%)

(1) 哪个电话是你的?

(2) 她是哪国人?

(3) 哥哥爱喝中国茶, 弟弟也喜欢喝中国茶。

(4) 我的好朋友叫英英, 她有两个弟弟。

(5) 我问你, 今年是二零零几年? 去年呢?

(6) 这个男老师是好老师吗?

(7) 上个星期六是谁的生日?

(8) 我的朋友很多, 有很多英国人, 没有中国人。

(9) 学生问老师:"你喜欢狗吗? 你有狗吗?"

(10) 这个美国男老师的英国女朋友有三只很小的中国狗。

(11) 爱去图书馆看书的那个中国人是我的中文老师。

(12) 我想开一个生日会，请朋友们来我家吃饭。
_____

(13) 我每天早上七点起床，八点吃早饭，九点开始上课。
_____

(14) 放学以后我和朋友一起去打篮球。
_____

(15) 我总是告诉爸爸妈妈学校的事情。
_____

3. Translate the following passages into English. (15%)

(1) 我生在英国，可是爸爸妈妈都是中国人，我的中文不好，因为我只能说一点儿，不能看，也不能写。我的妈妈常说："你应该学看中文书！"
_____
_____

(2) 我去年开始在学校学中文，教中文的是一个美国女老师，她是很好的老师。以前，她在北京学中文，现在她在英国教中文。
_____
_____

(3) 这个美国老师喜欢学外文，她会说很多外文，法文、日文她都会。每个星期我上三天中文课，星期一、星期三和星期五，每天一个小时。我很喜欢中文课，现在我可以和老师说中文，也可以写一点儿中文了。
_____
_____
_____

4. Translate the following into Chinese characters. (30%)

(1) What day is today?
_____

(2) I lived in Beijing before I lived in United Kingdom.
_____

(3) Who is your father's friend?
_____

(4) I don't have telephone, how about you?
_____

(5) How many days are there in a week?
_____

(6) They are my teachers, they are also my good friends.
_____

(7) British people like to drink tea in the morning.
_____

(8) Next Saturday is my birthday.
_____

(9) China is very beautiful!
_____

(10) That dog is not mine, this one is.
_____

(11) Who tells you that he is my younger brother?
_____

(12) I play tennis with my older brother every Saturday afternoon.
_____

(13) When we eat supper, we don't watch TV.
_____

(14) Our school has more than 200 foreign students.
_____

(15) The teacher who teaches Chemistry is Mr. Gao.
_____

5. Answer the following questions with Chinese characters. (10%)

(1) Q: 你家有几口人？他们是谁？
A: _____

(2) Q: 你喜欢什么运动？
A: _____

(3) Q: 你最喜欢什么课？
A: _____

(4) Q: 你为什么学中文？
A: _____

(5) Q: 在家的时候，你每天几点吃晚饭？
A: _____

Exercise Answers

Unit 1

Ex. 1.6

1. 日 sun   2. 月 moon   3. 马 horse   4. 儿 young boy   5. 家 home, family   6. 龟 tortoise
7. 火龙 fire dragon   8. 女人 woman   9. 儿子 son   10. 女儿 daughter   11. 子女 son and daughter
12. 家人 family member   13. 小牛 little bull   14. 小羊 little sheep   15. 山火 mountain fire
16. 火山 volcano   17. 大人 adult   18. 水牛 water buffalo   19. 山羊 goat   20. 人口 population

Ex. 1.8

1. C. Beijing   2. B. Shanghai   3. C. Tianjin   4. A. Chongqing
5. A. Lasa   6. B. Dunhuang   7. A. Xianggang   8. B. Aomen

Ex. 1.13

Beijing   (100083)   Shanghai   (201607)
Tianjin   (305896)   Chongqing (400825)
Lhasa   (850164)   Dunhuang   (736200)

Ex. 1.14 & 1.15

Pinyin Name	Country/City Name	Area Code	Pinyin Name	Country/City Name	Area Code
Xiānggǎng	Hong Kong	00852	Àomén	Macao	00853
Mǎláixīyà	Malaysia	0060	Yìndùníxīyà	Indonesia	0062
Fēilǜbīn	the Philippines	0063	Xīnjiāpō	Singapore	0065
Hélán	Holland	0031	Bǐlìshí	Belgium	0032
Pútáoyá	Portugal	00351	Xībānyá	Spain	0034
Ài'ěrlán	Ireland	00353	Yìdàlì	Italy	0039
Yīngguó	UK	0044	Zhōngguó	China	0086
Fǎguó	France	0033	Déguó	Germany	0049

Ex. 1.17

Country Name	Pinyin Name	Area Code	Area Code
Denmark	Dānmài	〇〇四五	0045
India	Yìndù	〇〇九一	0091

Nepal	Níbó'ěr	○○九七七	00977
Iran	Yīlǎng	○○九八	0098
Egypt	Āijí	○○二	002
Turkey	Tǔ'ěrqí	○○九	009
Pakistan	Bājīsītǎn	○○九二	0092
Iraq	Yīlākè	○○九六四	00964

Ex. 1.18

10 shí　　12 shí'èr　　14 shì　　15 shíwǔ　　19 shíjiǔ
20 èrshí　　36 sānshíliù　　44 sìshísì　　78 qīshíbā　　99 jiǔshíjiǔ

Ex. 1.20

月 moon　　口 mouth　　家 home, family　　四 four
日 sun　　子 son　　女 female　　龙 dragon
水 water　　儿 young boy　　龟 tortoise　　八 eight
火 fire　　人 people　　牛 bull, cow　　六 six
羊 sheep, ram　　天 sky　　五 five　　十 ten
马 horse　　小 small, little　　七 seven　　水牛 water buffalo
山 mountain, hill　　大 big　　九 nine　　火山 volcano

Ex. 1.22

1507895 一五〇七八九五　　51678259 五一六七八二五九　　8795429 八七九五四二九
2878960 二八七八九六〇　　45369788 四五三六九七八八　　2546987 二五四六九八七

Unit 2

Ex. 2.6

1. How do you do? I am Big Bull. 你好！我是大牛。
2. How do you do? I am Little Moon. 你好！我是小月。
3. She is Little Water. 她是小水。
4. He is Big Hill. 他是大山。

Ex. 2.10

I am…　　　　　　我是……
He is…　　　　　　他是……
I am called…　　　　我叫……
His surname is…　　他姓……
How do you do?　　你好！
She is Xiaoshui.　　她是小水。
I am English.　　　我是英国人。
You are Chinese.　　你是中国人。

Exercise Answers

Ex. 2.15

1.

| 他 | 是 | 英 | 国 | 人。|

2. 王家 Family Wang 小王 Little Wang (a young person) 国王 king 王国 kingdom
女王 queen 王子 prince 英国女王 GB's queen

Ex. 2.19

I, me	我	we, us	我们
you	你	you (plural)	你们
he, him	他	they, them (male)	他们
she, her	她	they, them (female)	她们

Ex. 2.20

我→我的   我们→我们的
你→你的   你们→你们的
他→他的   他们→他们的
她→她的   大中→大中的

Ex. 2.23

2. 英国 United Kingdom   英国人 British   美国 United States   美国人 American
美人 beauty   中国 China   电话 telephone   好人 nice person
好电话 nice phone   我的电话 my telephone

3. (1) We are British. 我们是英国人。
(2) She is Chinese. 她是中国人。
(3) They are American. 他们是美国人。
(4) His telephone is mine. 他的电话是我的。
(5) My telephone number is 0798 6784 2351 我的电话是〇七九八六七八四二三五一。

Unit 3

Ex. 3.4

	我	I, me
	爸爸	father
jiějie	姐姐	elder sister
gēge	哥哥	elder brother
	妈妈	mother
mèimei	妹妹	younger sister
yéye	爷爷	grandfather
nǎinai	奶奶	grandmother
	弟弟	younger brother

Ex. 3.12

1. 我姓王。 → 我不姓王。
2. 他叫马大山。 → 他不叫马大山。
3. 这是我哥哥。 → 这不是我哥哥。
4. 他是我爸爸。 → 他不是我爸爸。
5. 那是我妈妈。 → 那不是我妈妈。
6. 这是中国。 → 这不是中国。

Ex. 3.14

谁是英国人？ Who is English?
她是谁？ Who is she?
谁是小英的妈妈？ Who is Xiaoying's mother?
谁是中国人？ Who is Chinese?
谁是他的爸爸？ Who is his father?
他是谁？ Who is he?

Ex. 3.16

1. I am called Xiaoshui. 我叫小水。
2. A: Are you Xiaoying? B: No, I am not. A：你是小英吗？ B：不，我不是。
3. A: Is your surname Wang? B: Yes. A：你姓王吗？ B：是，（我姓王）。
4. He is Chinese. 他是中国人。
5. My father is not Chinese. 我爸爸不是中国人。
6. A: Are you Chinese? B: Yes, I am. A：你是中国人吗？ B：是，我是。
7. Who is Chinese? 谁是中国人？
8. Who is not Chinese? 谁不是中国人？
9. Who is your younger sister? 谁是你的妹妹？
10. Who is Xiaoying's elder brother? 谁是小英的哥哥？

Ex. 3.21

1. 我家有五口人。
2. 他有一个姐姐，没有妹妹。
3. 我妈妈有一个电话。
4. 这只英国狗大。
5. 那个中国人有两只狗。

Ex. 3.22

1. 这个人好，那个人不好。 This man is good, and that man is not good.
2. 这个电话好，那个电话不好。 This telephone is good, and that telephone is not good.
3. 这只狗大，那只狗不大。 This dog is big, and that dog is not big.
4. 英国狗大，中国狗不大。 British dogs are big, and Chinese dogs are not big.
5. 哥哥的狗大，我的狗小。 My elder brother's dog is big, and my dog is small.

Ex. 3.24

1. I have an elder sister. 我有一个姐姐。
2. My mum doesn't have a younger brother, but a younger sister. 我妈妈没有弟弟，她有一个妹妹。

3. These two English dogs are big. 这两只英国狗（很）大。
4. Does your younger sister have a dog? 你妹妹有狗吗？
5. My father has two telephones, one is good, and the other one is not good. 我爸爸有两个电话，一个好，一个不好。

Unit 4

Ex. 4.6

你是哪国人？　　　　　（哪国：which country）
你是中国哪儿人？　　　（哪儿：which place）
你姓什么？　　　　　　（什么：what）
你家有几口人？　　　　（几：how many）

Ex. 4.8

1. B. 英国人

> Listening script:
> A：你好，你是中国人吗？
> B：不是。
> A：你是美国人吗？
> B：我不是美国人，我是英国人。
> What is the nationality of the person?

2. B. 爸爸的哥哥

> Listening script:
> A：他是你爸爸吗？
> B：不是，他是我爸爸的哥哥。我爸爸是他的弟弟。
> Who is the man?

3. A. 三口人

> Listening script:
> A：你有姐姐没有？
> B：没有。
> A：你有妹妹吗？
> B：没有。
> A：你有没有哥哥？
> B：没有。
> A：弟弟呢？
> B：没有。我家有爸爸，妈妈，我。
> How many family members does she have?

Ex. 4.10

1. 他是中国人。　　→　　谁是中国人？

2. 小水的妈妈是英国人。 → 小水的妈妈是哪国人？
3. 小水的爸爸是中国Beijing人。 → 小水的爸爸是中国哪儿人？
4. 哥哥有两只狗。 → 哥哥有几只狗？
5. 他家有六口人。 → 他家有几口人？
6. 我姓王，我叫王小牛。 → 你姓什么？你叫什么？
7. 你是英国人。 → 你是英国人吗？
8. 我没有弟弟。 → 我没有弟弟，你呢？

Ex. 4.14
1. Her surname is Xiaomei. (×)
2. There are four people in her family. (×)
3. She has an older brother, and he is a university student. (√)
4. She has an older sister who is a middle school student. (×)
5. Her mother is a middle school teacher. (√)
6. Her father is also a teacher at middle school. (×)

Ex. 4.15
1. 爸爸的电话也很好。
2. 她也不是大学生。
3. 谁也有哥哥？
4. 我的老师也是美国人。
5. 他家也有四口人。

Ex. 4.25
1. I love to drink Chinese tea. 我爱喝中国茶。
2. My father drinks only very good English tea. 我爸爸只喝很好的英国茶。
3. I love my home very much. 我很爱我的家。
4. The male teacher loves his family very much. 男老师很爱他的家人。
5. America is very beauiful, American women are also pretty. 美国很美，美国女人也很美。

Unit 5

Ex. 5.6
1. B. 四月十号　　2. A. 一月七日　　3. C. 十月十三日
4. B. 六月十九号　　5. C. 四月五日

Ex. 5.9
1. My elder sister's birthday is on the 31st of December. 我姐姐的生日是十二月三十一号。
2. My friend, when is your birthday? 我的朋友，你的生日是几月几号？
3. She is my old friend, and she is also my very good friend. 她是我的老朋友，也是我的好朋友。

Ex. 5.14
星期一 Monday	一个星期 a week	一个星期一 a Monday
一个月 a month	一月 January	两个月 two months
一天 a day	一年 a year	两个星期 two weeks

Exercise Answers

水星 Mercury   火星 Mars   日期 date

Ex. 5.15
1. Friday, 12th of October, 2007 → 二零零七年十月十二号，星期五
2. Saturday, 24th of Novemer, 2007 → 二零零七年十一月二十四号，星期六
3. Friday, 2nd of May, 2008 → 二零零八年五月二日，星期五
4. Thursday, 25th of December, 2008 → 二零零八年十二月二十五号，星期四
5. Monday, 5th of January, 2009 → 二零零九年一月五号，星期一
6. Sunday, 21th of June, 2009 → 二零零九年六月二十一号，星期天

Ex. 5.16
1. A. 二零零六年   2. C. 星期日   3. C. 十二月
4. C. 八月十八日   5. A. 一九九七年七月七号   6. B. 一九一一年十月十日

Ex. 5.22
1. 一年有十二个月。 → 一年有多少个月？
2. 他家有六口人。 → 他家有几口人？
3. 哥哥有一只狗。 → 哥哥有几只狗？
4. 中国有很多人。 → 中国有多少人？
5. 我有二十五个老师。 → 你有多少个老师？

Ex. 5.25
1. 王老师爱喝茶。
2. 今天是你的生日吗？
3. 一年有多少个星期？
4. 这个星期六是谁的生日？
5. 今天是十一月二十八号，星期五。

Revision Unit 1

Character Revision
1. (1) good 好   mother 妈   elder sister 姐   she, her 她   younger sister 妹   surname 姓
   (2) ending particle for follow-up question 呢   ending particle for question 吗   which 哪
   (3) what 什   plural marker 们   you 你   he 他
   (4) who 谁   language, utterance 话
2. 爱   学   家
3. hero 英   tea 茶
   he 他   you 你
   call 叫   ask 问   which 哪
   yesterday 昨   tomorrow 明

175

Unit 6

Ex. 6.7

1. 西北 northwest　中东 Middle East　北美 North America　南美 South America
 这是北京，北京很大，有很多人。This is Beijing. Beijing is very big and has lots of people.
 那是东京，东京的中国人不多。That is Tokyo. Chinese people in Tokyo are not many.
2. (1) Where are you from?　你是哪国人？or 你是哪儿人？
 (2) I am from China. 我是中国人。
 (3) I am from Beijing, China. 我是中国北京人。
 (4) His father is from the UK. 他爸爸是英国人。
 (5) Her mother is from the United States. 她妈妈是美国人。

Ex. 6.12

1. 十一点半　六点十五（分）　一点四十五（分）　十点十五（分）
2. 九点半　两点十五（分）　五点四十五（分）　七点二十五（分）
3. 一点十分　七点二十五（分）　三点四十（分）　十一点十五（分）

Ex. 6.13

1. 十一点半/ 十一点三十(分)　　　2. 一点四十五(分)
3. 三点四十(分)　　　　　　　　4. 一点十分

Ex. 6.15

1. What time is it now? 现在几点？
2. It is half past twelve. 现在十二点半。or 现在十二点三十(分)。
3. It is ten to three. 现在两点五十(分)。

Ex. 6.22

	Chinese	English
1.	上个星期	last week
2.	这个星期	this week
3.	下个星期五	next Friday
4.	上个星期四	last Thursday
5.	这个月	this month
6.	上个月三号	the 3rd of last month
7.	下个月九号	the 9th of next month
8.	今天	today
9.	昨天	yesterday
10.	明天	tomorrow
11.	明天早上七点	7 a.m. tomorrow morning
12.	昨天晚上九点	9 p.m. last night
13.	今年	this year
14.	明年七月	July of next year
15.	去年六月	June of last year

Exercise Answers

Unit 7

Ex. 7.8
1. There are three people in my family: father, mother and me. 我家有三口人，爸爸、妈妈和我。
2. My father is English, and he likes to drink English tea. 我爸爸是英国人，他喜欢喝英国茶。
3. My mother is also English, but she doesn't like to drink tea. 我妈妈也是英国人，她不喜欢喝茶。
4. She likes to eat food and loves to eat both Chinese food and English food. 她喜欢吃饭，她爱吃中国饭，也爱吃英国饭。(or 她喜欢吃饭，中国饭、英国饭她都爱吃。)
5. I don't like tea. I only drink water. 我不喜欢茶，我只喝水。

Ex. 7. 23
1. My little brother likes to learn mathematics and chemistry. 我弟弟喜欢学数学和化学。
2. My Chinese language teacher is called Teacher Shi. 我的中文老师是时老师。
3. I have free time every Saturday afternoon. 我每个星期六下午都有时间。
4. He has English literature class at 10:30. 他十点半有英国文学课。

Unit 8

Ex. 8.5
1. 我下午喝英国茶。
2. 学生早上八点半来学校。
3. 他们现在不上课。
4. 爸爸星期六不吃中国饭。
5. 我家去年没有狗。or 去年我家没有狗。

Ex. 8.7
1. 我会说英文和中文。or 我会说中文和英文。
2. 我的校长每天下午五点半回家。
3. 这是你的时间表吗？

Ex. 8.12
1. 我喜欢喝茶。 → 我什么茶都喜欢喝。
2. 这个人会说外文。 → 这个人什么外文都会说。
3. 男老师不喜欢吃外国饭。 → 男老师什么外国饭都不喜欢吃。

Ex. 8.13

他的 his	哥哥的 elder brother's	姐姐的 elder sister's	弟弟的 little brother's
高的 tall one	小的 small one	好的 good one	不好的 bad one
中国的 China's	英国的 UK's	学校的 school's	我家的 my family's

学数学的 those who study Math　　　　有狗的 those who have dog(s)
喝英国茶的 those who drink English tea　　回家的 those who go back to home
天天学外文的 those who study foreign language everyday
不喜欢来学校的 those who don't like to come to school

Ex. 8.15
1. 爱吃中国饭的（人）是我哥哥。
2. 会说中国话的（人）是我的校长。
3. 有两只狗的（人）是我很好的朋友。

Ex. 8.20
图书馆的书 the library's book (books at library)
好看的人 a good-looking person
姓王的老师 the teacher who is surnamed Wang
说中文的校长 the headmaster who speaks Chinese
看书的王小姐 Miss Wang who is reading a book
不上课的学生 the students who don't have lessons
喜欢中文的马先生 the Mr. Ma who likes Chinese
爱吃中国饭的文太太 the Mrs Wen who loves eating Chinese food
来中国的朋友 (a) friend who comes to China
说英文的国家 the country that speaks English

Ex. 8.22
1. 王老师教数学。Teacher Wang teaches Math.
2. 学生喜欢学化学。Students like to learn Chemistry.
3. 妈妈不看书。 Mother doesn't read books.
4. 爸爸天天早上喝英国茶。Father drinks British tea every morning.
5. 星期六下午不上课。 There is no lesson on Saturday.
6. 我的校长会说外国话。 My headmaster can speak foreign language.
7. 他和朋友们一起吃中国饭。He and his friends have Chinese food together.

Unit 9

Ex. 9.8
1. My favourite sport is tennis. 我最喜欢的运动是网球。
2. I play tennis three days every week. 我每个星期打三天网球。
3. I play basketball with my friends every Saturday afternoon at 2:30. 我每个星期六下午两点半和朋友一起打篮球。

Ex. 9.13
因为新图书馆新书很多，所以学生们都喜欢去新图书馆看书。Since there are many new books in the new library, students all like to go to the new library to read books.
因为我喜欢看书，所以我有很多书。 Since I like reading, I have lots of books.
因为弟弟不是学生，所以他天天都有时间看电视。Since my little brother is not a student, he has lots of time to watch TV everyday.
因为他的爱好是运动，所以他每个星期六都打网球。Since his hobby is sports, he plays tennis every Saturday.
因为爸爸妈妈是中国人，所以我也是中国人。Since my father and mother are Chinese, I am also Chinese.

Exercise Answers

Ex. 9.15

1. 因为我是中学生，所以没时间看电视。 Since I am a secondary school student, I do not have time to watch TV.
2. 妹妹喜欢在家看电视。 My younger sister likes to watch TV at home.
3. 男学生都爱打篮球。 Boy students all like playing basketball.
4. 姐姐常常晚上在家看电视。 My elder sister often watches TV at home in the evening.
5. 你最喜欢什么运动? What's your favourite sport?

Ex. 9.22

1. I want to hold a birthday party at home. 我想在家开一个生日会。
2. I want to hold a birthday party this Sunday. 我想这个星期天开一个生日会。
3. Who wants to cook tonight? 今天晚上谁（想）做饭?
4. I don't know who cooks for us. 我不知道谁给我们做饭。
5. Please give the teacher a call tonight. 今天晚上请给老师打（一个）电话。

Unit 10

Ex. 10.5

1. 我知道他会说英国话。 I know he can speak English.
2. 每个人都喜欢那个男学生。 Everyone likes that boy student.
3. 这儿人人都有电视。 Here, everyone has a TV.
4. 他总是做好吃的饭。 He always makes delicious food.
5. 中学生（星期六和星期天）不忙。 Secondary school students are not busy (on Saturdays and Sundays).

Ex. 10.7

1. 王老师想教两年的数学。
2. 弟弟天天晚上看一个半小时的电视。
3. 我们每个星期上三个小时的英文课。
4. 我七月去北京学一个月的中文。
5. 我每天下午在图书馆看一个小时的书。

Ex. 10.12

我小的时候　when I was little
我十岁的时候　when I was ten years old
三月的时候　when (it is in) March
二零零三年的时候　when (it is in the) year 2003
看电视的时候　when (sb.) watches TV
吃饭的时候　when (sb.) eats a meal
回家的时候　when (sb.) returns home
不想打网球的时候　when (sb.) doesn't want to play tennis

Ex. 10.14

1. When I was 10 years old, I didn't like to read (books). 我十岁的时候，不喜欢看书。
2. When it is 8 o'clock, I go to school. 八点的时候，我去学校。

3. When we eat supper, we don't watch TV. 我们吃晚饭的时候，不看电视。
4. While mother is cooking, my younger sister and I read books. 妈妈做饭的时候，（我）妹妹和我看书。
5. Give him a little water to drink. 给他一点儿水喝。

Ex. 10.19

能	néng	can
可以	kěyǐ	may
应该	yīnggāi	ought to; should
喜欢	xǐhuān	like to
爱	ài	love to
想	xiǎng	want/plan to
会	huì	can, will

Ex. 10.21
1. 美国中学生最爱/喜欢/会打篮球。
   Secondary students in the United States love/like/are good at playing basketball.
2. 他会/能/可以说一点儿中文，你会/能/可以说中文吗?
   He can speak a little Chinese, can you speak Chinese?
3. 我爸爸妈妈是中国人，所以我应该/想/会学一点儿中文。
   My parents are Chinese, therefore I should/want to/will learn some Chinese.
4. 你可以/应该早一点儿回家。
   You may/should go back home a bit earlier.
5. 我朋友想以后去中国学中文。
   My friend wants to study Chinese in China in the future.

Revision Unit 2

Character Review

1. 常　完　写
2. capital 京　　　　　　tall 高
   road 道　　　　　　　this 这
   teach 教　　　　　　 number 数　　　　do 做
   meal 饭　　　　　　 restaurant 馆
   because 因　　　　　country 国
   think 想　　　　　　 busy 忙　　　　　always 总
   time, room 间　　　　ask 问
   speak, say 说　　　　lesson, class 课
3.

Character	Pinyin	Meaning	Refers to
跃	yuè	jump, leap	跳高 tiàogāo, high jump

Exercise Answers

踢	tī	kick	足球 zúqiú, football, soccer
跑	pǎo	run	马拉松 mǎlāsōng, marathon
搏	bó	fight	击剑 jījiàn, fencing
划	huá	row	皮划艇 píhuátǐng, canoeing 赛艇 sàitǐng, rowing
举	jǔ	lift	举重 jǔzhòng, weightlifting
投	tóu	throw, hurl	标枪 biāoqiāng, javelin 铅球 qiānqiú, shot put
射	shè	shoot	射箭 shèjiàn, archery 射击 shèjī, shooting
跳	tiào	jump	跳远 tiàoyuǎn, long jump
骑	qí	ride	自行车 zìxíngchē, bicycle 马术 mǎshù, equestrianism
游	yóu	swim	游泳 yóuyǒng, swimming

Appendix I Vocabulary

Pinyin	Chinese Characters	Meaning	Unit
niú	牛	bull, cow	1.3
guī	龟	tortoise	1.3
huǒ	火	fire	1.3
jiā	家	home, family	1.3
mǎ	马	horse	1.3
rì	日	sun, day, date	1.3
shān	山	mountain, hill	1.3
shuǐ	水	water	1.3
yáng	羊	sheep, ram	1.3
yuè	月	moon, month	1.3
dà	大	big	1.3
ér	儿	young boy	1.3
kǒu	口	mouth; a measure word	1.3
nǚ	女	famale	1.3
rén	人	people	1.3
tiān	天	heaven, sky, day	1.3
xiǎo	小	little, small	1.3
zhōng	中	middle, centre	1.3
zǐ	子	son, boy	1.3
bā	八	eight	1.4
èr	二	two	1.4
jiǔ	九	nine	1.4
líng	〇	zero	1.4
liù	六	six	1.4
qī	七	seven	1.4
sān	三	three	1.4
shí	十	ten	1.4
sì	四	four	1.4
wǔ	五	five	1.4
yī	一	one	1.4

Appendix I Vocabulary

Pinyin	Chinese Characters	Meaning	Unit
Dàzhōng	大中	Dazhong (a boy's name)	2.1
hǎo	好	good, fine	2.1
nǐ	你	you	2.1
nǐ hǎo	你好	how do you do	2.1
shì	是	be (am, is, are)	2.1
tā	他	he, him	2.1
tā	她	she, her	2.1
wǒ	我	I, me	2.1
Xiǎoshuǐ	小水	Xiaoshui (a girl's name)	2.1
guó	国	kingdom, state	2.2
jiào	叫	be called	2.2
wáng	王	king; a common surname	2.2
Wǒ jiào Mǎ Dàzhōng.	我叫马大中。	I am called Ma Dazhong.	2.2
Wǒ jiào Xiǎoshuǐ.	我叫小水。	I am called Xiaoshui.	2.2
Wǒ shì Dàzhōng.	我是大中。	I am Dazhong.	2.2
Wǒ shì Yīngguórén.	我是英国人。	I am British.	2.2
Wǒ shì Zhōngguórén.	我是中国人。	I am Chinese.	2.2
Wǒ xìng Wáng.	我姓王。	My surname is Wang.	2.2
xìng	姓	surname	2.2
yīng	英	hero, bravery	2.2
Yīngguó	英国	United Kingdom	2.2
Zhōngguó	中国	China	2.2
de	的	possessive particle ('s)	2.3
diàn	电	electricity, tele-	2.3
diànhuà	电话	telephone	2.3
huà	话	speech, sayings, language	2.3
měi	美	beautiful	2.3
men	们	plural marker (for pronoun)	2.3
wǒmen	我们	we, us	2.3
wǒmen de	我们的	ours	2.3
bàba	爸爸	father	3.1

Pinyin	Chinese Characters	Meaning	Unit
dìdi	弟弟	younger brother	3.1
jiārén	家人	family members	3.1
māma	妈妈	mother	3.1
nà/nèi	那	that; so; in that case	3.1
zhè/zhèi	这	this	3.1
bù	不	no, not	3.2
bú shì	不是	am/is/are not	3.2
gēge	哥哥	elder brother	3.2
jiějie	姐姐	elder sister	3.2
ma	吗	ending particle for a question	3.2
mèimei	妹妹	younger sister	3.2
shéi/shuí	谁	who, whom	3.2
dà gǒu	大狗	big dog	3.3
ge	个	individual; a common measure word	3.3
gǒu	狗	dog	3.3
liǎng	两	two (of)	3.3
liǎng zhī gǒu	两只狗	two dogs	3.3
méi	没	negative marker for 有	3.3
méiyǒu	没有	not have	3.3
wǔ kǒu rén	五口人	five family members	3.3
yī ge jiějie	一个姐姐	an elder sister	3.3
yǒu	有	have	3.3
yǒu méiyǒu	有没有	do (you) have…?	3.3
zhī	只	single; a measure word for small animal	3.3
jǐ	几	how many/much	4.1
jǐ kǒu rén	几口人	how many family members	4.1
nǎ	哪	which	4.1
nǎguó	哪国	which country	4.1
nǎguó rén	哪国人	people from which country	4.1
nǎr	哪儿	where	4.1
ne	呢	how about…?	4.1

Appendix I Vocabulary

Pinyin	Chinese Characters	Meaning	Unit
nǐ jiā ne	你家呢	how about your family	4.1
shénme	什么	what	4.1
dàxué	大学	university	4.2
dàxué lǎoshī	大学老师	university teacher	4.2
dàxuéshēng	大学生	university student	4.2
lǎo	老	old	4.2
lǎoshī	老师	teacher	4.2
shī	师	master	4.2
xiǎoxué	小学	primary school	4.2
xiǎoxuéshēng	小学生	primary school student	4.2
xué	学	learn, study	4.2
xuésheng	学生	student	4.2
yě	也	also	4.2
zhōngxué	中学	secondary school	4.2
zhōngxué lǎoshī	中学老师	secondary school teacher	4.2
zhōngxuéshēng	中学生	secondary school student	4.2
ài	爱	love; love to	4.3
chá	茶	tea	4.3
érzi	儿子	son	4.3
hē	喝	drink	4.3
hěn	很	very	4.3
nán	男	male	4.3
nán lǎoshī	男老师	male teacher	4.3
nán xuésheng	男学生	boy student	4.3
nánren	男人	man	4.3
nǚ lǎoshī	女老师	female teacher	4.3
nǚ xuésheng	女学生	girl student	4.3
nǚ'ér	女儿	daughter	4.3
nǚrén	女人	woman	4.3
zhī	只	only	4.3
èrshísì rì/ hào	二十四日/号	the 24th of (month)	5.1

Pinyin	Chinese Characters	Meaning	Unit
hào	号	date, number	5.1
hǎo péngyou	好朋友	good friend	5.1
jǐ hào	几号	which day	5.1
jǐ yuè	几月	which month	5.1
jǐ yuè jǐ hào	几月几号	which month and which day	5.1
nǚ péngyou	女朋友	girl friend	5.1
péngyou	朋友	friend	5.1
shēng	生	give birth; person	5.1
shēngri	生日	birthday	5.1
èr líng líng bā	二零零八	2008	5.2
èr líng líng jiǔ	二零零九	2009	5.2
jīn	今	now, present	5.2
jīnnián	今年	this year	5.2
jīntiān	今天	today	5.2
líng	零	zero	5.2
nián	年	year	5.2
qī	期	date	5.2
shí'èr yuè	十二月	December	5.2
xīng	星	star	5.2
xīngqī	星期	week	5.2
Xīngqītiān	星期天	Sunday	5.2
Xīngqīyī	星期一	Monday	5.2
yī yuè	一月	January	5.2
zhè ge yuè	这个月	this month	5.2
dàyuè	大月	big month	5.3
duō	多	many, much	5.3
duōshao	多少	how many/much	5.3
míng	明	brightness	5.3
míngnián	明年	next year	5.3
míngtiān	明天	tomorrow	5.3
nǐ wèn wǒ	你问我	you ask me	5.3
qù	去	go to	5.3

Appendix I Vocabulary

Pinyin	Chinese Characters	Meaning	Unit
qùnián	去年	last year	5.3
shǎo	少	few	5.3
wèn	问	ask	5.3
wǒ wèn nǐ	我问你	I ask you	5.3
xiǎo yuè	小月	small month	5.3
zuó	昨	the recent past	5.3
zuótiān	昨天	yesterday	5.3
běi	北	north	6.1
Běijīng	北京	Beijing (capital of China)	6.1
dōng	东	east	6.1
dōngběi	东北	northeast	6.1
dōngnán	东南	southeast	6.1
jīng	京	capital (city)	6.1
nán	南	south	6.1
Nánjīng	南京	Nanjing (city of China)	6.1
xī	西	west	6.1
xīběi	西北	northwest	6.1
xīnán	西南	southwest	6.1
bàn	半	half	6.2
diǎn	点	o'clock, point	6.2
fēn	分	minute	6.2
jǐ diǎn	几点	which o'clock; what time	6.2
liǎng diǎn	两点	two o'clock	6.2
shíyī diǎn	十一点	eleven o'clock	6.2
shíyī diǎn bàn	十一点半	eleven thirty	6.2
sìshíwǔ fēn	四十五分	forty-five minutes	6.2
xiàn	现	at present	6.2
xiànzài	现在	now	6.2
xiànzài jǐ diǎn	现在几点	what time is it now	6.2
zài	在	be in/ at/ on	6.2
shàng	上	up, top	6.3

Pinyin	Chinese Characters	Meaning	Unit
shàngwǔ	上午	a.m. (8a.m.–12p.m.)	6.3
wǎn	晚	late	6.3
wǎnshang	晚上	evening (6p.m.–)	6.3
wǔ	午	noon	6.3
xià	下	under, below	6.3
xiàwǔ	下午	p.m. (2–6p.m.)	6.3
zǎo	早	early	6.3
zǎoshang	早上	morning (before 8a.m.)	6.3
zhōngwǔ	中午	midday (12–2p.m.)	6.3
bàn ge	半个	half (of)	7.1
chī	吃	eat	7.1
chī fàn	吃饭	eat a meal	7.1
dōu	都	all	7.1
fàn	饭	cooked rice; meal, cuisine	7.1
hē chá	喝茶	drink tea	7.1
hé	和	and	7.1
huān	欢	love, joy	7.1
rénrén	人人	everyone	7.1
tiāntiān	天天	everyday	7.1
xǐ	喜	be fond of; happiness	7.1
xǐhuān	喜欢	love, like	7.1
Xīngqīliù	星期六	Saturday	7.1
bā bǎi	八百	800	7.2
bǎi	百	hundred	7.2
bàn tiān	半天	half day	7.2
dàjiā	大家	everyone	7.2
èrshí jǐ	二十几	20+	7.2
kè	课	class, lesson	7.2
měi	每	every	7.2
měi ge xīngqī	每个星期	every week	7.2
shàng	上	attend (class)	7.2

Appendix I Vocabulary

Pinyin	Chinese Characters	Meaning	Unit
shāng kè	上课	start/attend class	7.2
suì	岁	year of age	7.2
wài	外	foreign	7.2
wàiguó	外国	foreign country	7.2
xià kè	下课	finish class	7.2
yǒude	有的	some	7.2
biǎo	表	chart, table, watch	7.3
huà	化	change, culture	7.3
huàxué	化学	chemistry	7.3
jiān	间	a unit (of time, space)	7.3
méiyǒu shíjiān	没有时间	do not have time	7.3
shí	时	time; also use as a surname	7.3
Shí lǎoshi	时老师	Teacher Shi	7.3
shíjiān	时间	time	7.3
shíjiānbiǎo	时间表	timetable	7.3
shù	数	number	7.3
shùxué	数学	mathematics	7.3
wàiwén	外文	foreign language	7.3
wén	文	language; literary; use as a surname	7.3
Wén lǎoshi	文老师	Teacher Wen	7.3
wénhuà	文化	culture	7.3
wénxué	文学	literature	7.3
Yīngguó wénxué	英国文学	English literature	7.3
Yīngwén	英文	English language	7.3
yǒu shíjiān	有时间	have time (free)	7.3
Zhōngwén	中文	Chinese language	7.3
huí	回	return	8.1
huì	会	can, will	8.1
huí guó	回国	go (back) to one's home country	8.1
huí jiā	回家	go (back) home	8.1
huì shuō	会说	can speak	8.1

Pinyin	Chinese Characters	Meaning	Unit
lái	来	come	8.1
Rìwén	日文	Japanese language	8.1
shuō	说	speak, say	8.1
wàiguóhuà	外国话	foreign language	8.1
xiào	校	school	8.1
xiàozhǎng	校长	headmaster/ mistress	8.1
xuéxiào	学校	school	8.1
zhǎng	长	head, chief	8.1
Zhōngguóhuà	中国话	Chinese language	8.1
gāo	高	tall, high; a surname	8.2
jiāo	教	teach	8.2
kě	可	but; may, can	8.2
kěshì	可是	but, however	8.2
qǐ	起	a group, get up	8.2
tài	太	great, too	8.2
tàitai	太太	Mrs.	8.2
xiān	先	first; precede	8.2
xiānsheng	先生	Mr.	8.2
xiǎojie	小姐	Miss	8.2
yìqǐ	一起	together	8.2
kàn	看	read, see, look, watch	8.3
kàn shū	看书	read book(s)	8.3
fànguǎn	饭馆	restaurant	8.3
guǎn	馆	hall, gallery	8.3
lǎo shū	老书	old book(s)	8.3
shū	书	book(s)	8.3
tú	图	picture, map	8.3
túshū	图书	maps and books	8.3
túshūguǎn	图书馆	library	8.3
wàiwénshū	外文书	foreign language book(s)	8.3
xīn	新	new	8.3
xīn lái de	新来的	newly arrived	8.3

Appendix I Vocabulary

Pinyin	Chinese Characters	Meaning	Unit
xīn shū	新书	new book(s)	8.3
àihǎo	爱好	hobby	9.1
dǎ	打	play, fight, do, strike	9.1
dǎ qiú	打球	play ball games	9.1
dòng	动	move	9.1
lánqiú	篮球	basketball	9.1
lánzi	篮子	basket	9.1
qiú	球	ball	9.1
wǎng	网	net, web	9.1
wǎngqiú	网球	tennis	9.1
yùn	运	revolve	9.1
yùndòng	运动	sports	9.1
zuì	最	the most/-est	9.1
cháng	常	frequently; a surname	9.2
chángcháng	常常	often	9.2
dào	到	till; arrive	9.2
diànshì	电视	television	9.2
kàn diànshì	看电视	watch TV	9.2
kěyǐ	可以	may	9.2
shì	视	vision	9.2
suǒ	所	that which; all that	9.2
suǒyǐ	所以	therefore	9.2
wèi	为	for; on account of	9.2
wèishénme	为什么	why	9.2
xiǎoshuō	小说	novel	9.2
yǐ	以	give cause; consider	9.2
yīn	因	cause, reason	9.2
yīnwèi	因为	because	9.2
zài jiā	在家	at home	9.2
dào	道	say; truth	9.3
dōngxi	东西	thing	9.3

Pinyin	Chinese Characters	Meaning	Unit
gěi	给	for, give	9.3
hǎochī	好吃	delicious	9.3
kāi	开	hold, open; turn on	9.3
kāi shēngrìhuì	开生日会	hold a birthday party	9.3
méi rén	没人	nobody	9.3
qǐng	请	invite; please	9.3
shēngrìhuì	生日会	birthday party	9.3
xià ge Xīngqītiān	下个星期天	next Sunday	9.3
xiǎng	想	want/plan to; miss	9.3
zhī	知	know; knowledge	9.3
zhīdào	知道	know	9.3
zuò	做	do, make	9.3
zuò fàn	做饭	cook food	9.3
chuáng	床	bed	10.1
fàng	放	release, put	10.1
fàngxué	放学	release from (finish) school	10.1
hòu	后	afterwards, behind	10.1
máng	忙	busy	10.1
qǐ chuáng	起床	get up (from bed)	10.1
shàng kè	上课	attend class	10.1
shàng xué	上学	attend school	10.1
yǐhòu	以后	afterward; in the future	10.1
yíhuìr	一会儿	(for) a while	10.1
zǒng	总	anyway; general, main	10.1
zǒngshì	总是	always	10.1
de shíhou	…的时候	when…; while…	10.2
diǎn	点	a tiny amount; o'clock	10.2
gào	告	tell, sue	10.2
gàosu	告诉	tell	10.2
hou	候	timing, weather; wait	10.2
qíng	情	affection, feeling	10.2

Appendix II Extra Vocabulary

Pinyin	Chinese Characters	Meaning	Unit
shénme shíhou	什么时候	when	10.2
shì	事	matter, fact, event	10.2
shíhou	时候	time	10.2
shìqing	事情	issue, matter	10.2
shuō huà	说话	talk	10.2
sù	诉	tell; go to court	10.2
wán	完	finish, complete	10.2
yìdiǎnr	一点儿	a little; some	10.2
yǒushíhou	有时候	sometimes	10.2
Běijīng Dàxué	北京大学	Peking University	10.3
gāi	该	should; ought to	10.3
kāishǐ	开始	start (work)	10.3
kěnéng	可能	maybe, possible	10.3
néng	能	can; ability, power, energy	10.3
qián	前	(vs. 后) in front of ; forward; preceding	10.3
qiánnián	前年	the year before last	10.3
qiántiān	前天	the day before yesterday	10.3
shǐ	始	a beginning	10.3
xiǎoshí	小时	(an) hour	10.3
xiě	写	write	10.3
yīng	应	should; ought to	10.3
yīnggāi	应该	should; ought to	10.3
yǐqián	以前	in the past; before	10.3

Appendix II Extra Vocabulary

Pinyin	Chinese Characters	Meaning	Unit
yéye	爷爷	grandfather	3.1
nǎinai	奶奶	grandmother	3.1
niúnǎi	牛奶	milk	7.1
qìshuǐ	汽水	fizzy drinks	7.1
shuǐ	水	water	7.1

Pinyin	Chinese Characters	Meaning	Unit
kělè	可乐	Coca-Cola	7.1
guǒzhī	果汁	juice	7.1
jiǔ	酒	alcohol drinks	7.1
píjiǔ	啤酒	beer	7.1
hōngjiǔ	红酒	red wine	7.1
báijiǔ	白酒	white wine	7.1
kāfēi	咖啡	coffee	7.1
lìshǐ	历史	History	7.3
dìlǐ	地理	Geography	7.3
wùlǐ	物理	Physics	7.3
shēngwù	生物	Biology	7.3
tǐyù	体育	P.E.	7.3
Fǎwén	法文	French	7.3
yìshù	艺术	Art	7.3
yīnyuè	音乐	Music	7.3
(dǎ) páiqiú	(打)排球	(play) volleyball	9.1
(dǎ) pīngpāngqiú	(打)乒乓球	(play) table tennis	9.1
(dǎ) yǔmáoqiú	(打)羽毛球	(play) badminton	9.1
(dǎ) gǎnlǎnqiú	(打)橄榄球	(play) rugby	9.1
yóuyǒng	游泳	swim	9.1
pǎobù	跑步	run	9.1
(tī) zúqiú	(踢)足球	(play) football	9.1

Appendix III Fixed Expressions

Chinese Characters	Pinyin	Meaning	Unit
你好!	Nǐ hǎo!	How do you do! / Hello!	1
再见!	Zàijiàn!	Goodbye.	1
谢谢!	Xièxie!	Thank you.	1
欢迎!	Huānyíng!	Welcome!	1
早!	Zǎo!	Morning.	2

Appendix III Fixed Expressions

Chinese Characters	Pinyin	Meaning	Unit
早上好！	Zǎoshang hǎo!	Good morning.	2
下午好！	Xiàwǔ hǎo!	Good afternoon.	2
晚上好！	Wǎnshang hǎo!	Good evening.	2
不用谢！	Bú yòng xiè!	You are welcome!	2
你好吗？	Nǐ hǎo ma?	How are you?	3
我很好，谢谢！	Wǒ hěn hǎo, xièxie!	I am fine, thank you.	3
你家人好吗？	Nǐ jiārén hǎo ma?	How is your family?	3
很好，谢谢。	Hěn hǎo, xièxie.	(They are) Fine, thanks.	3
请进！	Qǐng jìn!	Come in, please.	4
请坐！	Qǐng zuò!	Sit down, please.	4
请喝茶！	Qǐng hē chá!	Please have some tea.	4
你多大？	Nǐ duō dà?	How old are you?	5
你今年多大？	Nǐ jīnnián duō dà?	How old are you this year?	5
你属什么？	Nǐ shǔ shénme?	What is your Chinese Zodiac animal?	5
我属X。	Wǒ shǔ X.	My Chinese Zodia animal is X.	5
祝你生日快乐！	Zhù nǐ shēngrì kuàilè!	Happy birthday to you!	5
太好了！	Tài hǎo le!	Great!	6
真棒！	Zhēn bàng!	Fantastic!	6
请问，厕所在哪儿？	Qǐng wèn, cèsuǒ zài nǎir?	Excuse me, where is the lavatory?	6
对不起，我不知道。	Duìbuqǐ, wǒ bù zhīdào.	I am sorry, I don't know.	6
你几点上课？	Nǐ jǐ diǎn shàng kè?	When does your class start?	7
你几点下课？	Nǐ jǐ diǎn xià kè?	When does your class end?	7
今天你有几节课？	Jiāntiān nǐ yǒu jǐ jié kè?	How many hours of class do you have today?	7
今天晚上你有没有时间？	Jiāntiān wǎnshang nǐ yǒu méiyou shíjiān?	Do you have time tonight?	7

Chinese Characters	Pinyin	Meaning	Unit
谁教你们数学？	Shuí jiāo nǐmen shùxué?	Who teaches you Math?	8
你去不去图书馆？	Nǐ qù bu qù túshūguǎn?	Do you go to the library?	8
我们一起去图书馆吧！	Wǒmen yìqǐ qù túshūguǎn?	Let's go to library together!	8
请问……	Qǐngwèn…	Please may I ask…	9
你喜欢运动吗？	Nǐ xīhuan yùndòng ma?	Do you like sports?	9
你喜欢什么运动？	Nǐ xīhuan shénme yùndòng?	Which sport do you like?	9
你会不会打网球？	Nǐ huì bu huì dǎ wǎngqiú?	Can you play tennis?	9
我们认识一下，我是……	Wǒmen rènshi yí xià, wǒ shì…	Let me introduce myself, I am…	10
我来介绍一下，这是……	Wǒ lái jièshào yí xià, zhè shì…	Let me make introduction, this is…	10
我会说一点儿中文。	Wǒ huì shuō yìdiǎnr zhōngwén.	I can speak a little Chinese.	10
祝你快乐！	Zhù nǐ kuàilè!	Wish you happiness!	10
新年快乐！	Xīnnián kuàilè!	Happy New Year!	10

Appendix IV List of Chinese Characters

Pinyin	Chinese Characters	Meaning
ài	爱	love; love to
bā	八	eight
bà	爸	father
bǎi	百	hundred
bàn	半	half; semi-, hemi-
běi	北	north
biǎo	表	a (time) watch; a grid table

Appendix IV List of Chinese Characters

Pinyin	Chinese Characters	Meaning
bù	不	not, no (a negative marker)
chá	茶	tea
cháng	常	frequently, often
chī	吃	eat
chuáng	床	bed
dǎ	打	hit, beat, play (games), make (call)
dà	大	big, large
dào	到	(from ...) to; until; arrive
dào	道	way, road, method
de	的	of; processive marker ('s)
dì	弟	younger brother
diǎn	点	point, dot, o'clock
diàn	电	electricity, tele-
dōng	东	east
dòng	动	move; movement
dōu	都	all
duō	多	many, much, more
ér	儿	son, child
èr	二	two
fàn	饭	meal, food; cooked rice
fàng	放	set free; put; let go
fēn	分	separate; cent (money); minute (of time or degree)
gāi	该	should; ought to
gāo	高	high; height
gào	告	tell, inform, sue
gē	哥	elder brother
gè	个	general measure word
gěi	给	give; to, for (sb. do something)
gǒu	狗	dog
guǎn	馆	hall
guī	龟	turtle, tortoise

197

Pinyin	Chinese Characters	Meaning
guó	国	kingdom, nation, country, state
hǎo	好	good, nice, fine, well
hào	号	day (of the month), number
hē	喝	drink
hé	和	and, with; together with; harmony
hěn	很	very
hòu	后	after, behind
hòu	候	wait, await; timing, weather
huà	话	speech, sayings, language
huà	化	change, civilize, culture
huān	欢	happy, joyous, merry; lively
huí	回	return, go or come back; turn around
huì	会	can, will; know (a language); be able to; meeting
huǒ	火	fire
jǐ	几	several; how many/much
jiā	家	family, home
jiān	间	among, between; classifier for space and time
jiào	叫	be called; shout, yell
jiāo	教	teach, instruct
jiě	姐	elder sister
jīn	今	present-day, now; modern, contemporary
jīng	京	national capital
kāi	开	open, turn on (a light, etc.); operate (a machine, etc.)
kàn	看	look, see, read, visit; call on (friends, etc.)
kè	课	lesson, class
kě	可	possibly; may, can
kǒu	口	mouth; a measure word
lái	来	come
lán	篮	basket
lǎo	老	old, aged

Appendix IV List of Chinese Characters

Pinyin	Chinese Characters	Meaning
liǎng	两	two (of)
líng	零	zero; fragments
liù	六	six
lóng	龙	dragon
ma	吗	question particle for a question
mā	妈	mother
mǎ	马	horse
máng	忙	busy
me	么	suffix (like 什么，这么)
méi	没	not (have); have not
měi	美	beautiful, pretty, good
měi	每	each, every
mèi	妹	younger sister
men	们	plural marker of noun or pronoun
míng	明	bright, clear; birghtness; know, understand
nà	那	that; so; in that case
nǎ	哪	which
nán	男	male, man
nán	南	south
ne	呢	ending particle for a question marker
néng	能	can; ability, power, energy
nǐ	你	you
nián	年	year
niú	牛	ox, bull
nǔ	女	woman, female
péng	朋	friend (as in 朋友)
qǐ	起	begin to; start to ... (verb suffix); rise; stand up
qī	七	seven
qī	期	term; the period of time
qián	前	in front of; ahead; front, before
qíng	情	affection, emotion, passion, situation

Pinyin	Chinese Characters	Meaning
qǐng	请	ask, request, invite; please
qiú	球	sphere, globe, ball
qù	去	go to
rén	人	person, people
rì	日	day, sun
sān	三	three
shān	山	mountain, hill
shàng	上	up; on top of
shǎo	少	few, little, less
shēng	生	give birth to; live, life, person
shī	师	teacher, master
shí	十	ten
shí	什	what
shí	时	time
shǐ	始	begin, start; beginning
shì	是	be (am, is, are)
shì	视	vision; look at; examine, regard, consider, inspect
shì	事	affair, matter, thing
shū	书	book
shù	数	number
shuǐ	水	water, rivers
shuí/shéi	谁	who, whom
shuō	说	speak, say, explain, scold
sì	四	four
sù	诉	tell, inform; go to court
suì	岁	year (old); year of age
suǒ	所	therefore; all that
tā	他	he, him
tā	她	she, her
tài	太	greatest, highest; too, excessively
tiān	天	day, sky; the heavens

Appendix IV   List of Chinese Characters

Pinyin	Chinese Characters	Meaning
tú	图	picture, drawing, illustration, diagram, chart, map
wài	外	outside; foreign, external
wán	完	finish, complete (the action of the preceding verb)
wǎn	晚	night, evening; late (in time)
wáng	王	king; Wang (a common surname)
wǎng	网	net, web
wèi	为	for; on account of
wén	文	culture, writing, composition; literary language
wèn	问	ask, inquire
wǒ	我	I, me
wǔ	五	five
wǔ	午	noon
xī	西	west
xǐ	喜	be happy; happiness; be fond of
xià	下	under, below
xiān	先	earlier, first
xiàn	现	present, current; now; at the time
xiǎng	想	intend; want/plan to; would like to; miss
xiǎo	小	small, little
xiào	校	school, institute
xiě	写	write, compose
xīn	新	new, modern
xīng	星	star
xìng	姓	surname
xué	学	learn, study
yáng	羊	sheep, ram
yě	也	also, too; as well
yī	一	one
yǐ	以	give cause; consider; in order to
yīn	因	because; because of; on account of

Pinyin	Chinese Characters	Meaning
yīng	英	hero, bravery; person of outstanding ability
yīng	应	should, must; ought to
yǒu	有	there be; have, possess
yǒu	友	friend, ally; friendly
yuè	月	month, moon
yùn	运	revolve; motion
zài	在	be in/at on; exist
zǎo	早	early morning; early; in advance; beforehand
zhǎng	长	head, chief, person in charge
zhè	这	this
zhī	知	know, understand, realize, inform; knowledge
zhī zhǐ	只	measure word for animal only
zhōng	中	middle, centre; in the middle of
zǐ	子	son, child, person
zǒng	总	general, main
zuì	最	the most/-est (prefix for the superlative)
zuó	昨	yesterday; in the past; formerly
zuò	做	make, work, do; act as